Open Heart, Open Mind

CLARA HUGHES

Published by Simon & Schuster

New York London Toronto Sydney New Delhi

Simon & Schuster Canada
A Division of Simon & Schuster, Inc.
166 King Street East, Suite 300
Toronto, Ontario M5A 1J3

This book is published independently by the author and publisher. It has no connection to, affiliation with, or endorsement by any of the entities, including corporate, sporting, or individual, or any of their products, which the book may depict or refer to.

Chapter 15 of *Open Heart, Open Mind* includes re-worked material by Clara Hughes first published in "On Top of the World" in *Canadian Cyclist* magazine in 2003, with kind permission of CanadianCyclist.com.

This Simon & Schuster Canada edition January 2017

For information about special discounts for bulk purchases, please contact Simon & Schuster Special Sales at 1-800-268-3216 or CustomerService@simonandschuster.ca.

SIMON & SCHUSTER CANADA and colophon are registered trademarks of Simon & Schuster, Inc.

Library and Archives Canada Cataloguing in Publication

Hughes, Clara, author
    Open heart, open mind / Clara Hughes.
Reprint of: Open heart, open mind / Clara Hughes.—Toronto : Simon
    and Schuster Canada, 2015.
ISBN 978-1-4767-5699-8 (paperback)
    1. Hughes, Clara. 2. Hughes, Clara—Mental health. 3. Women
Olympic athletes—Canada—Biography. 4. Women speed skaters—Canada—
Biography. 5. Women cyclists—Canada—Biography. 6. Depressed persons—
Canada—Biography. I. Title.
GV697.H84A3 2016   796.092   C2015-908160-2

Interior design by Akasha Archer

Manufactured in the United States of America

10 9 8 7 6 5 4 3 2 1

ISBN 978-1-4767-5698-1
ISBN 978-1-4767-5699-8 (pbk)
ISBN 978-1-4767-5700-1 (ebook)

This book is written for anyone who has struggled or is struggling. And it is written for all those connected to the struggle. It was written with the hope that knowing something of my life's journey, what's really behind my public smile, might inspire others to embark on their own liberating paths.

CONTENTS

RECYCLING 2010–2012

LIVING IN A PERMANENT OFF-SEASON

VANCOUVER OLYMPICS 2010

1

WITH GLOWING HEARTS

It started with my being asked to be the flag-bearer. I was sure I had the capacity to carry our flag and still perform. My first race was thirty-six hours after the march into BC Place, but I wasn't concerned. Without hesitation, I accepted. The Vancouver Winter Games in 2010 were my fifth games. I thought I'd been through it all but competing at home took the stress to a new level. I was propelled from the hermetic existence of training and became, for a few days, the single focus of the biggest sporting event in Canadian history.

Richmond City Hall became Olympic central for the press conference. The secrecy surrounding the identity of the flag-bearer ended there on January 29, 2010. I stood at the top of an ornate staircase that wound down to a sea of newspaper reporters, TV media crews, politicians, Olympic officials, teammates, and citizens. I felt an elation equalling my best athletic moments. For the first time in my life, I felt that bliss without having to skate or ride myself through a world of pain.

The press conference turned my elation to despair. All my confidence and excitement was shattered as soon as I entered the obligatory media scrum. Reporters asked about the flag-bearer curse, the cost of venues, and protests on the streets. Anchor Wendy Mesley jokingly introduced me as "a hard-drinking . . . troublemaker" on CBC's *The National*.

I had no idea that after agreeing to carry my country's flag I'd be expected to be an expert on all things Olympic, but I tried to answer all the controversial questions as well as I could.

I left the press conference in a state of shock. I'd made a mistake and a big one at that. There was no way out, and I knew it. My fifth Olympic Games had begun.

I sat alone in the apartment that'd been provided as part of our home-team advantage. My husband, Peter, set it up and made sure I had everything I needed to succeed, but I knew none of this would help with how I was feeling. I opened my laptop to write my coach an e-mail, thinking she'd have some solid advice. That's when I saw an e-mail from my good friend Tewanee Joseph.

Tewanee was the CEO of the Four Host First Nations (FHFN), made up of the Lil'wat, Musqueam, Squamish, and Tsleil-Waututh First Nations. Every Olympic moment would take place on their territorial land. I'd met him a few years earlier when looking for a connection to the Olympics deeper than sport. I'd sent him a note asking for his help in connecting me with the First Nations youth. I wanted to share the Olympics with them and, in turn, feel a connection to their beautiful land.

His e-mail was an invitation to a brushing-off ceremony. While all my competitors moved deeper into bubbles that isolated them from everything but sport, Peter, a few of my closest support staff, and I travelled to find out exactly what this ceremony was.

Tewanee's home was on the small patch of Squamish First Nations Reserve on Vancouver's North Shore. We walked into the warmth of the house, greeted by an abundance of food and smiles. All offered warm hugs; all were eager to make us welcome. After having been more or less institutionalized through a program of elite training, not to mention the pressure I put on myself, I was relieved to relax and forget my responsibilities.

These feelings strengthened when Tewanee's wife, Rae-Ann, gave me a silver hummingbird pendant her son had picked out for me. She told me it would give me wings to fly. I wore it the entire Games.

The brushing-off ceremony was conducted amid candles, singing, and chanting, with kids laughing and playing in the background. An elder addressed us in his native language. His gestures and soothing voice, like the tones of Mother Nature, made me feel he was telling the story of the earth, wind, sun, and rain. I sat smiling with the others, taking in the energy and the calmness of his voice, and feeling completely within the moment.

Another elder addressed each of us in turn, opening our hearts to the energy of the flame and brushing away negativity. He told us, "I cannot heal you of your pain. Only you can heal yourself with your open heart and your open mind."

At one point, Tewanee's thirteen-year-old daughter stood in the middle of the room, crying. Though my friends and I didn't know what was happening, we listened respectfully as the elders told her, "Thank you for sharing your beautiful tears with us. Let them flow."

Since I knew I carried a pool of raw feelings and unshed tears inside of me, I was grateful to see such despair welcomed as powerful and good.

One of the elders spoke to me in English: "You can only attract success for yourself if you want every single one of your competitors to be good and strong. When you wish good things for others, this comes back to you. The strength to be kind is not often asked for, but this is perhaps the most important strength to have."

The elder then addressed Peter and my team: "You are Clara's force field, her circle of strength—there to support her. She needs you." They all turned their eyes toward me. I felt utterly loved.

The stress of bearing the flag and competing melted away. I left armed with clarity, ready for the Games, our Games.

As host nation, Team Canada would be the last of eighty-two nations to enter the stadium. That meant a long, restless wait. There were 206 of us in our red jackets, impatiently watching the ceremony on our cellphones, hearing the boisterous cheers as the crowd welcomed each team—Albania and Ghana and Ethiopia with only 1 member each, the United States with 215.

Now, it was Team Canada's turn to cross the threshold into the expanse of BC Place. I could see little soap bubbles falling like snow from the sky, a magical faux-winter wonderland in the unfathomable hugeness of the stadium.

I examined my flag holster with belated concern: Did I use one hand or two to insert the pole? No one had explained any of this to me. As the gap widened between the rest of the team and me, I felt stranded, but the faces around me were alight with the wonder of the moment.

A volunteer yelled: "Take the flag!" He thrust it into my hand, then counted down: "Five, four, three, two . . ."

I was ordered to march, but before I did, I took a moment to look up at the perfect red-on-white maple leaf, waving like one of nature's own on a late fall Manitoba day.

I held up our flag, proudly, for the whole world to see, knowing that as our country's flag-bearer, I had become something much bigger, stronger, and more beautiful than just me. I remembered the motto of these Games: With Glowing Hearts. And realized: *This is it.*

2

THE RACES

February 13

With the Opening Ceremony over, I was just another athlete. I focused on my primary task—excellence for Canada, for my teammates, for myself.

I hadn't been skating anywhere near my ability. After winning gold in the 5000-metre race at the 2006 Torino Olympics, I had barely qualified for Team Canada. I knew I was capable of something special. I just had to find it.

A speed skater's stride is a fragile thing. Sometimes you own it for a day, a week, a month, or a season. Then you lose it and spend a day, a week, a month, or a season trying to find it again, fighting yourself until a fog of self-doubt smothers every part of your life.

Now, each time I took to the ice, I was looking for that precious, elusive form in which skating becomes beautiful. I wanted to be like my teammate Kristina Groves, with her big, effortless corner strides, or Christine Nesbitt, with her reckless abandon, during which she pushes, head to toe, with every ounce of muscle fibre she possesses.

I felt disconnected from the perfection that I knew lay dormant inside me, killing any chance of moving freely on my seventeen-inch blades. I was looking for a magical solution, forgetting that all I needed was to stop overthinking my every move, to just let my body flow.

So as not to be thrown off balance by the crowd's intensity, I went to the oval to watch the men's 5000 metres. From high up in the stadium, the skaters in their shiny, bright skin suits looked like figures zipping about in a video game. When I saw Lee Seung-hoon, the South Korean skater, dancing around the oval's turns to win silver, I was blown away by his technique. So was my coach, Xiuli Wang (pronounced Ju Li Wong). Grabbing my arm, she exclaimed, "Look at that guy. He's like a running man!"

After the crowd left the oval, and the TV lights had been turned off, those of us racing the next day began our practice. When I stepped onto the ice, I remembered Lee, skating so relaxed, imprinting his movements over my own familiar blueprint, and now gliding fast and easy.

Xiuli yelled, "Running-man arm!" Her voice echoed around the empty stadium, which a few hours before had roared with cheers. "Whatever you're doing, just keep doing it. Don't think about it."

February 14: My first race—the 3000 metres

When I arrived at the oval, a few crazy Canadians were already in the stands. For the seventeen days of the Games, hockey fans would morph into speed-skating fans, luge fans, bobsled fans, all-around Olympics fans. Some had painted their faces with maple leaves. A few were yelling, "Go, Clara!"

I couldn't acknowledge them, because I didn't want to risk turning this 3000-metre race into a social event. I had to focus on the moment.

In our change room, I wrestled into the exclusively designed, high-tech skin suit—no easy task!—then put on my toque and the glasses that stopped my eyes from watering.

I inked between my left thumb and forefinger the four powerful words given to me by the Squamish elder: *Open Heart, Open Mind*. I wanted to see these words while stretching. While looking at my watch. While warming up on the stationary bike. While attaching sensors to my ankles to record the instant I crossed the finish line.

I hit the ice feeling anxious, but aggressive and ready. I was paired with Maren Haugli from Norway, the result of a random draw. We would be skating 7.5 laps, counterclockwise around the 400-metre oval. To equalize our distance, we would change lanes from outer to inner in the backstretch every lap. Though physically we were racing against each other, we were actually racing against the clock.

The rink went silent as we positioned ourselves on the start line. My confidence bordered on the terrifying, I felt so much power. Later, my massage therapist, Shayne Hutchins, would say that I looked like a Winnipeg street fighter, with an open switchblade in my hand, ready to cut someone.

The pistol fired.

A scream burst from the fans—a scream that would follow us around the oval. Knowing how loud the crowd could be, Xiuli and I had set up a code. Arms moving one way told me one thing; arms moving another way told me something else.

The Richmond Olympic Oval was so alive it felt like it had a heartbeat. Though I didn't dare glance up, I could hear every single voice, every cheer, every stomp of every foot, every clap of every hand. It fueled me.

When I heard the bell signalling the final lap, I thought, *No, I want more! I don't want to stop.*

I had skated 4:06, putting me in second place. And I wasn't even exhausted. When my teammate Kristina Groves took to the ice, I cheered for her the entire 7.5 laps, because I wanted her to be great, even if she knocked me off the podium. That was what happened. After Kristina's brilliant performance, she held third while I was in fourth. We huddled on the bench, in joy and torment, watching the scoreboard. I slipped to fifth, but I didn't care. I was thirty-seven years old, and I had skated one of the best races of my life.

Kristina won bronze by one-hundredth of a second. The crowd exploded for her. Though I knew I couldn't have skated faster, I knew I could have skated farther. I had wanted five more laps. In eleven days, I would get them. *My* race, *my* distance—the 5000 metres.

February 15–23

When I wasn't training, I was revelling in the Games with my husband, Peter, who was staying with me in the apartment across from the oval. As we travelled around the city, we could feel the adrenaline in the air as awareness of the enormity of these Olympics took hold. People stopped me in the streets to tell me I'd made them feel proud to be Canadian. And I had only finished fifth! They had seen Kristina and me share the joy of her bronze, and they had connected to that moment.

Eyes glued to the TV screen, I watched moguls skier Alex Bilodeau, poised on his hilltop, so determined and pure, ready to win Canada's first gold in Vancouver. I watched Britt Janyk ski the race of her life but finish sixth. I watched the skeleton winner, Jon Montgomery, the crazy, bearded Manitoba lumberjack, strut through the streets of Whistler, pounding back a pitcher of beer. And then there was Joannie Rochette, bravely skating to bronze in memory of her mother, who'd suffered a fatal heart attack days before.

These Games offered so much to cheer, so much to admire, so much to love, yet I could not forget Nodar Kumaritashvili, the young Georgian luger, who had crashed during a high-speed practice run before the Opening Ceremony. The sight of Nodar's lifeless body, sprawled like a rag doll on the guardrail, which I had seen live on TV, had imprinted itself on my heart, as it had on so many others. It made me want to honour Nodar by carrying his spirit with me and by skating the best races of my life.

Peter and I became so full of the Games—the winning and the losing, the tension and the celebrations and the heartbreak—that we had to escape our apartment. After a walk through the park across the street, we were drawn, once again, to the TV in a hotel lobby. Tessa Virtue and Scott Moir were floating across the ice en route to another Canadian gold.

I noticed a familiar face in the lobby—Gaétan Boucher!

Gaétan was the reason I had taken up speed skating. At age sixteen, while channel-surfing on my mom's TV, I had watched, spellbound, as he attacked his last race at the 1988 Calgary Olympics. It's hard to exaggerate the impact of that transformative moment. I was an unruly teenager, a real troublemaker, smoking a pack a day, doing soft drugs, drinking anything raw and straight, and partying a lot. As I absorbed Gaétan's intensity, his power, his elegance, I connected to speed skating's beautiful movement, and I knew: *Someday I'm going to skate for Canada.*

Now, here I was, actually doing it, actually living that dream.

Gaétan called to me, "So, are you ready, Clara?"

I answered him in my awestruck, sixteen-year-old rebel's voice, "Fuck, yeah!"

February 24

My nerves woke me sooner than I wanted. My bedroom had been customized with blackout curtains, hung by Peter, and a special Swedish bed, so that until now I'd had some of the best sleeps of my life. I glanced at the clock—5:40 A.M. Since my race wasn't until 1:00 P.M., I had just over seven hours to endure, somehow. All 565 square feet of my apartment seemed to shrink around me, creating claustrophobia.

After four Olympics, I shouldn't have been nervous, but I was. The more I tried to calm myself, the more panicky I felt. The previous night's random draw had told me that I'd be skating before all of my fastest competitors. I would be the one setting the pace, then having to wait to see if I could hold my place.

With my eyes watering, I made my four-shot Americano espresso in my Saeco coffee machine, but I couldn't stomach it. Anyone who knows how much I love my coffee would understand this was serious. I tried to eat some steel-cut oatmeal with a sliced banana, but couldn't do that either. I was lonely for Peter, who was staying at a hotel. Mentally preparing for a big race is a solitary exercise.

Coaches advise us to treat Olympic races like any others, but they are not like any others, and all races are torturous. Even though I'm a creature of endurance, I still shudder at the agony I experience skating all-out for 5000 metres. I especially dread facing that excruciating barrier of pain in the last third of the race. No matter how hard I work out in the weight room, or run, or skate, nothing ever prepares me for how deeply I will be forced to tap into my reserves. And so, in the still-dark hours before what I knew would be my final Olympics as a speed skater, I paced and worried, then slept fitfully till a sliver of light peeked through a gap in the curtains at 7:40 A.M.

Only five more hours. Five hours to find balance. To be motivated, yet relaxed. To rest enough, but not too much. To eat enough, but not overdo it. To watch enough of the Olympics to remain connected, but not so much that I lost concentration.

I have seen Olympic competitors collapse under pressures that broke their spirits in ways that couldn't be fixed. I also knew that giving up, at any point in my career, would have opened up the option of quitting every time I felt a task was too hard.

My process—my success—came from forcing myself to face my own doubts, then to empower myself by conquering them. This meant diving into the darkest corner of my spirit and asking myself: *Do you have what it takes? Do you still have what other people believe you have?* These questions are terrifying, yet inspiring. So often they have spurred me out of pessimism, releasing me to fly. Something happens deep in my brain, like the flipping of a switch, and then I'm ready to do the impossible.

While I was searching for something to bring me to the necessary focus, I remembered an e-mail that my friend Hubert Lacroix, president of the CBC, had sent to me:

> So here it is. The end of your latest four-year journey to skate the perfect race, to find a place, a state of mind and body, of speed and strength, of concentration and execution where only you can go because of all the meticulous preparation, every day for the last four years. Actually for as long as you have skated. You know that. The women who skate against you know that. They know that you can take the pain and not flinch. They see that in your eyes. Let them see that. It scares them. This is your advantage.

I wrote out the entire e-mail—six pages in my notebook—letting the words sink deep into my psyche. I drank my coffee. I ate my breakfast. I took a nap. I watched more of the Olympics, and then I left for the rink.

As I closed the apartment door, I remember thinking, *When I return, it will be all over. What's it going to be?*

Every day at the venue, I had signed programs, chatted with volunteers, and posed for pictures, as requested. On this day, everyone was quiet, not wanting to disturb me. When I greeted a few people, they beamed back. An RCMP officer exclaimed, "Today's the day, kiddo. You get 'em."

I assured him and myself I would.

After a full warm-up on the ice, then a cooldown, I followed the timetable written on a torn scrap of paper I'd put in my pocket.

12:25 P.M. massage
12:35 P.M. bike warm-up
1:00 P.M. skin suit on
1:08 P.M. go to infield
1:10 P.M. warm-up drills on infield
1:26 P.M. put on skates
1:30 P.M. go onto ice
1:40 P.M. race!

I went through my routine, wanting both to savour and to remember every moment, reminding myself: *No more speed skating after today. This is it!*

The ice had just been cleaned and flooded. I would be racing in the first pair. *Will the surface have hardened enough? Will it be harder for the last pairs, giving them an advantage?* It didn't matter; I was ready to skate on jelly or on concrete.

Once on the infield, I was hit by the tumult of shouting fans: "Go, Canada! Go, Clara!" Canada was on fire, having already won more medals in Vancouver than at any other Games.

During my last brief warm-up, I felt the thousands of hours of practice effortlessly flowing through me. When the referee's whistle called me to the line, I glanced at my hand to see *Open Heart, Open Mind,* like a kid cheating on an exam. I felt fierce, as if I was ready to step onto a battlefield, but it wasn't another competitor I had to face down. I needed to persuade my body to endure a nearly unbearable amount of self-inflicted pain.

I was paired with Masako Hozumi of Japan, just as I had been the previous year in a World Cup event in Russia. I remembered the quick turnover of her blades—*toock toock toock toock*—sounding like the metronome that when I was a kid had forced me to play my piano scales faster and faster, creating anxiety. That's how I'd felt throughout that entire race, even though Masako was always behind me. My own pacing was more deliberate—*dook, dook, dook.* I stopped myself from fussing. *It is what it is.*

At the start line, Masako said, "Good luck, Clara."

I remembered the message of the elder: *You can only attract success for yourself if you want your competitors to be strong.* I wished Masako luck, and I meant it.

I planted my front blade perpendicular to the start line, angled my back blade to it, then crouched in a coiled position, ready to strike as I had tens of hundreds of times before, using my core muscles to lift my weight and to stabilize myself. A speed skater is never so alone as when waiting for the gun. Despite the support of a nation, I felt naked in that moment.

I will never forget the sound of the starting gun.

Usually it takes me two laps to get up to speed. This time, as I found my pace, I unexpectedly felt so relaxed, so fluid, as if the motion was happening through me. I could see the lap times, but the numbers meant nothing to me. They were just shapes. The cheers of the crowd drowned out the sound of Masako's skates, but I didn't fully let the spectators in because I knew I'd need them later.

I was alone after three laps, Masako far behind. Toward the end of the race, I started hearing the crowd become louder and louder. As Xiuli mimed her instructions, she looked like a bird attempting to take flight. I mentally cheered. *That's my coach!*

The crowd was thunderous. Since I wasn't hurting, I told myself to push harder, but not so hard as to sabotage my form and rhythm, which still felt free and good. It was a strange battle for me. I was so used to the pain of racing that now I had to fight just to let myself feel good, but not so good that I fell into a trance. I was inside every stride. Skating had become a dance. I had achieved the mental state called "easy speed," which means I felt as if I was going slowly while skating at maximum capacity.

With three laps to go, I fuelled myself with the roar of the crowd. When I came to the last corner on the outer track, with one lap to go, I let out this "Yeahhh!" It just burst from me—an almost primal release.

I shot down the final straightaway with my eyes on the finish line and my brain shouting, *You did it!*

I crossed the line, completely immersed in the moment, having forgotten about the finishing time. It hadn't seemed to matter, but there it was: 6:55.73. I had set a track record by three seconds, beating the best skate so far that day by more than eleven seconds.

Cruising to a stop, I screamed at the top of my lungs, letting the race come out of me—the race that had been lying dormant inside me my whole life. It was finally out. I felt this rapture, this joy, this satisfaction that I had achieved my ultimate goal, which was to feel every cell of my brain and my body working together in synchronized, pure, efficient perfection. It brought me back to seeing Gaétan Boucher for the first time and being hypnotized by the sheer power and elegance of his stride. Now, I had actually captured those moments for myself.

People in the stands were shouting, leaping from their seats, and high-fiving. I hugged everyone in sight—volunteers, friends, Xiuli, other coaches. At the same time, I thought, *Man, I'm going to look like a jerk if I end up in ninth place after this.*

The bizarre part was that I hadn't had to push myself to total exhaustion. I had felt that elusive perfection only four or five times in ten years, and it had happened at the Olympics on my home turf, for my last speed-skating race. *Had I metabolized the energy of every Canadian embracing the Games?*

After I settled down, I watched the other pairs compete. I saw myself bumped down to second, then to third. And that's where I held.

Bronze.

Someone handed me a Canadian flag. I jogged a lap of the infield, once again proudly waving the red-and-white for all to see. Even though the Czech skater Martina Sáblíková had won gold, I knew I was the person for whom everyone was cheering.

I saw my mom in the crowd, with Peter. I blew them both a kiss. My mom smiled with tears in her eyes. Earlier that year, she'd prom-

ised, "I'm going to be at your last race in Vancouver, no matter what."
She had missed all of my Olympic skating events out of concern for
my dad, even though they'd lived separately for three decades and were
now divorced.

I had fifteen minutes, after the flower ceremony, to return to my
apartment—escorted by two military guards—and change for the medal
ceremony. As I burst through the door, I shouted into the empty apartment, "I'm back! And I fucking did it!"

I picked up the telephone to dial my dad in Winnipeg.

After a few rings, he answered. "Whaaat?"

He sounded incoherent.

"Dad, it's Clara."

"Who? Who is this? Who are you?"

"Dad, it's your daughter, it's Clara."

"Oh, yeah, yeah, yeah."

"Did you see the race?"

"What? What are you talking about?"

"The Olympics. I just raced. Did you see how it went?"

"No, I went out for a walk. I was out."

"I got a bronze medal, Dad. I did a really good race. It was my best
race."

"Oh, yeah, yeah, yeah," he mumbled. "Of course. Yeah."

Disappointed, I hung up, then took a deep breath, reminding myself: *You can't fix it. Don't try.*

Because my father was a chronic alcoholic, I was used to incoher-
ence. I didn't realize that this once-brilliant man was now suffering
geriatric dementia. My dad had been confused, not loaded.

WINNIPEG
1972–1990

3

OUR HOUSE

My dad, Kenneth James Hughes, didn't know how to be a father, because during his childhood his own father had always been working down the coal mines or at the pub. When dealing with our family, my dad was often an angry drunk. The history of alcoholism went back to both of my grandfathers. Some little thing would trigger him, and if my mom opposed him, he'd become angrier. I grew up listening to my dad constantly yelling at my mom. Twice, he walked out on us at Christmas.

As a kid, you just try to survive. You grind whatever awful things you're experiencing into dust as they're happening. Sometimes I'd hide in the darkness of the closet with my hands over my ears and with my eyes pressed shut. I didn't understand that my father was an alcoholic, or even that he was drunk. I just knew he was angry. He was angry for reasons I didn't know, and since he was yelling at my mom, I guessed it was her fault.

One night, my mom made this really beautiful dinner—roast beef, potatoes, gravy, carrots—and my dad came home late. He screamed at her, a black and visceral scream unlike any I'd ever heard before. This time, when he threatened to leave, my mom opened the door. "Okay, go."

I believe my dad thought she'd change her mind, but she didn't. My mom had finally come to the end of what had seemed like infinite patience. She told him, "No more."

When my dad moved into his own apartment, I was nine and my sister, Dodie, was two years older. My parents never explained the separation to us, although it was obvious from the fury in our home why they needed to break up. Mom told us we could see our dad any time we wanted, and we were like, "Oh, cool, we'll have two homes."

I was relieved my dad had left, but nothing was ever the same after that.

I was born September 27, 1972, and I grew up on Riverton Avenue in Elmwood, a working-class residential area of Winnipeg. Our stucco bungalow was modest, like the others in the neighbourhood, with a finished attic, where my sister and I had our bedrooms. Hers faced the street, mine Elmwood Cemetery, which was like our neighbourhood park.

My dad was a big man in every way—six-foot-four with a huge head and lots of hair. His hands were also big, and his grip strong. Though he wasn't an athlete, he was like a polar bear in the water, joyfully lifting my sister and me high above the rough waves of Lake Winnipeg. That was during the happy times at Winnipeg Beach, where our family sometimes rented a little shack—you couldn't call it a cottage, and certainly not a summer home.

My father was an English professor at St. John's College, which is part of the University of Manitoba. It was a job he held for twenty-three years. To Ken Hughes, literature was like a religion. He covered every aspect of it, from art to psychology. He also published a slew of books, some exploring language—how words are used and why—and others on Manitoba artists and their works. All I knew as a kid was that we had thousands of books stashed all over our house.

My mother, Maureen, was beautiful, with two braids to her waist and granny glasses, like an artist-hippie. A Diane Keaton in her Woody Allen days. Before my father left, she was a stay-at-home mom who made everything from scratch—French bread, cinnamon rolls, croissants, all our birthday cakes. I didn't know prepackaged food existed until I saw a strange box in a friend's kitchen. *What? There's something called "brownie mix"?*

The law in our home was for Dodie and me to be seen and not heard. We avoided getting into trouble at all costs, even though we secretly found trouble all the time. My dad's mindset was a proper British one, where noise, yelling, even loud laughter were banned, along with bad words, though he said them all the time when he was drunk. The punishment in our family was the Belt, administered by my dad—not often, but always a possibility—so we lived in fear in some ways. I remember, once, my sister and me falling into a fit of uncontrollable laughter in a downtown restaurant where our family had ordered food. When we couldn't stop, my father insisted that we go home. We didn't even get to eat our hamburgers, and, yes, we got the Belt.

Our mealtimes were often fraught with tension. Since my dad liked to cook, he often made dinner. Dodie and I loved it when he made roast beef and Yorkshire pudding, but we hated his concoctions of liver, lima beans, and green peppers. Sometimes we'd have to sit at the table for hours, not allowed to leave until we finished everything. We used to hide food between the books on nearby shelves, so that when my dad moved them for one of his many renovations, he found shrivelled-up meals between the covers.

Dodie and I didn't like my mother's cooking either. It was too healthy. What we craved was junk food. Our sheepdog, Chaucer, the top dog on our street, sometimes helped us out with table scraps, as did our second sheepdog, Molly. Molly disappeared one day after she bit both Dodie and me in the face. My sister had to have stitches. We'd both received what we deserved because we used to torment Molly. I remember putting my face close to hers and growling fiercely. My mom still insists Molly went to a farm.

Because of the rules in our house, my sister and I were used to playing quietly together. Though our parents were frugal when it came to store-bought toys, my mom made sure we had lots of materials to build forts, to paint, to draw, always encouraging our creativity. She also read to us before we learned to read ourselves. I remember that we had several Barbie dolls, and I constructed little houses for them. One Christmas, my mom gave us each a box of clothes she had handmade for the dolls. I also remember that my sister and I cut off their hair and coloured their heads with markers. Our environment was always shifting, so it felt natural to reinvent Barbie.

Dodie and I were also supplied with plenty of costumes for dress-up—an activity that spilled out into the neighbourhood. Though traffic was busy around our house because of the Henderson Highway, the street was quiet at the other end, where we paraded in our costumes. I remember fighting over everyone's favourite—the "genie" costume, based on the TV show *I Dream of Jeannie*.

I don't remember much about Lord Selkirk Elementary School, except that I passed everything, and that I had many friends, since I've always been adaptable. I wasn't very respectful of my teachers, and I recall one saying to me in disgust, "Oh, you're going to be just like your sister!" By then, Dodie was beginning to rebel, and I remember thinking, *You want trouble? I'll give you trouble!* but I was never as bad as I wanted to be, even with Dodie as a role model.

I started playing sports when I was six, mostly community club stuff, like softball, soccer, and ringette, which resembles ice hockey but uses hollow, lightweight sticks to control a blue rubber ring. I played because I liked to play, and because it took me out of myself and away from home. Though I was able to hold my own in any sport that I tried, I was never the best.

My parents always encouraged me to do anything I wanted, but both strongly favoured the arts over sport. As a kid, I took piano, ballet, and art lessons. I was too big for ballet, and my fingernails were too long for the piano. That was my idea. My piano teacher was always trying to get me to cut them.

My dad listened to classical music and jazz on CBC radio, often with our canary, Shakespeare, singing along. Dodie and I were allowed to watch only one TV show a day, and my favourite was *The Love Boat*. Yup. *The Love Boat*.

Our family had two season tickets for the ballet, the symphony, and the opera, and we took turns attending. Because my dad had quit driving after his eighth accident, we rode the bus. I felt proud standing beside him at the stop, in my big fur coat with my little beret. I really looked up to my dad despite his flaws. I enjoyed it when it was just Dad and me, because I wanted so much to be like him.

At the concert hall, I wasn't enthralled by the music or the production, but I did have fun watching the stage through my green-and-gold opera glasses. More important, I loved the row of soda pops and the fact I could get refills at intermission. We weren't allowed anything so decadent at home. Afterward, when my dad and I went to Junior's restaurant, my life felt almost normal, but because he was so volatile, I was never sure how the day would end.

Artists loved my father because of his passion for the arts, and he was always adding to his massive art collection, so I grew up attending openings of artists like Bill Lobchuk at the Ukrainian Cultural Centre. Once again, I was mostly fixated on whether I would get a bottle of 7-Up; however, observing creative people possessed by a burning commitment to do what they loved had a fundamental impact on me.

My dad's consuming love of culture was a mystery, given his background. He was born in 1932 in the Midlands village of Langold, near Worksop, Nottinghamshire. His father, who'd been a coal miner from the age of twelve, didn't want either of his two sons to go down into the pit. Though there wasn't a book or a painting in my dad's house, as a teenager he would sit alone in their fancy parlour—traditionally used only for funerals and weddings—listening to opera on the radio and dreaming up a different world. His family thought he was crazy.

After serving for five years as a mechanic in the Royal Air Force, mostly in the Middle East, Kenneth Hughes immigrated to Montreal in 1956, at the age of twenty-three.

My mother grew up in Montreal, under the spell of her mother, Dodie, a lively and exuberant artist who lived to be ninety-six. After World War I, Dodie was a student at L'École des Beaux-arts de Montréal, then worked as a commercial artist. My mom's dad—Thomas Walton McBride, known as Tommy or TW—was a charming and persuasive salesman for the Rapid Grip and Batten lithography company. He was also an alcoholic. One Christmas Eve, he set fire to his car in their driveway. My mom remembers watching it burn from her window, then returning to bed to wait for Santa.

In 1938, when my mom was born, Dodie divorced Tommy. She celebrated by painting the living room deep rose and turquoise and getting pink broadloom. Dodie then moved to Toronto, leaving her three kids with Tommy and his mother. My mom attended Montreal West

High School. Afterward, she learned shorthand and typing, then took a job at a big New York ad agency, where her father had some influence. That happened in 1959.

Ten years after my grandparents' divorce, my grandmother married a sailor from Alabama, who was much younger. After that, she insisted my mother call her Dodie, because she thought it made her seem more youthful. Tommy also married again, and divorced again, and went through two formal detox treatments. When those failed, he became a transient and died alone in his fifties in a Toronto rooming house. Even though he wasn't religious, he'd raised money for Christian charities and was well loved, so many people attended his funeral.

Big Dodie (not to be confused with *Little* Dodie, my sister) was the only grandparent I knew. She was a colourful and forceful presence in my life. In 2005, she moved into our family home to be cared for by my mother. During one of my visits home, I suggested to Big Dodie that we paint together.

We both painted the same tulips.

Big Dodie, who had been legally blind for decades, created a beautiful abstract, so free and loose and lovely. I, a hobby artist who'd taken a few adult watercolour classes, attempted to be perfect, instead of letting the colours flow. That was one of my favourite experiences with Big Dodie, whom I remember every day. This is partly because Peter and I have so many dishes and pieces of pottery that she made, partly because I inherited her red hair, partly because she showed me how to be attractive, and partly because she was such a delightful, defiant original.

My mother and father met at one of Big Dodie's many parties, after she'd returned to Montreal from Toronto. My mother, who was visiting from New York, found herself chatting amiably to a tall, quite trim, and very fit man who was introduced to her as Kenneth Hughes. He was working at Dun & Bradstreet, sniffing out credit information for businesses. It was one of an assortment of jobs he'd had. They were two very good-looking people, with my dad seven years older. He was attracted to my mom's creative nature and artistic background. She found him fun and beguilingly curious about the world. He also rode an old Triumph TD motorcycle.

My mom moved back to Montreal, mostly because of her interest in my dad. She easily landed another secretarial job. Following a brief courtship, they were married in a simple ceremony, with a reception back at my dad's Ville de Brossard house in Greater Montreal. One evening, my mom noticed my father was very, very low in spirits because of his job. When she asked him what he'd like to do with his life, he replied with gratitude, "No one has ever asked me that before." He told her he wanted to further his education. She assured him she would support his dream.

Dad took a year of high school to make up all the grades he'd missed, then studied for four years as a mature student at Concordia University. After acquiring his master's at McGill, he enrolled in a doctorate program in Durham, England. Because this was 1967—Canada's centennial year—our country hosted cultural events in Britain, where my mom and dad met novelist Margaret Laurence, also from Manitoba. She introduced them to poet Al Purdy and his wife, Eurithe, resulting in friendships that endured after all of them returned to Canada.

On my parents' last night in England, their Oxford friends gave them a big farewell party; it was July 20, 1969, the day Neil Armstrong landed on the moon.

According to my mother, my father's alcoholism took hold when they were in Britain. Pub culture attracted him, and he fell into the habit of drinking every night. My mother, who is moderate in every way, was more bored at this point than alarmed.

By the time I entered the scene, my father's alcoholism was entrenched. At the core of his dissatisfaction seemed to be some confusion over his doctoral thesis. In the summer of 1969, he was advised by Durham University that his thesis had been rejected. After revision, it was turned down a second time. Since Kenneth Hughes knew himself to be a true scholar, he felt deeply wronged. He began drinking more heavily, transforming into a different person.

In retrospect, I believe my dad had a personality disorder. Perhaps he was bipolar, or a functional depressive, conditions no one talked about in those days. In later years, I remember letters and packages addressed to "Dr. Hughes," so I assume that's what he started calling himself.

Whether he simply thought he deserved that title, or whether he was delusional, I don't know.

My dad was a master of destruction in so many ways. He was constantly renovating—the result of a busy mind that kept him rearranging until everything was upside down. He built, then rebuilt, then rebuilt again. A closet became a bedroom, which became a bathroom. He turned the garage into a study. He constructed a platform for his bed, put up doors and partitions, then took them down again. His thousands of books had to be stacked and restacked every time he pulled out his sledgehammer. This created constant upheaval, constant interruptions in our living space, both reflecting and contributing to our family's instability.

Years later, after Peter and I moved into our first house in Quebec, I ripped out a stair railing, then left it lying around, with other random, incomplete construction projects. Peter finally said, "Just stop. If you're going to start something, you have to finish it." That made me aware that I was doing exactly what my dad had done. Fortunately, Peter curtailed the impulse.

As a kid, I liked to cook with Dad, and for a while I was convinced I was going to be a chef. But even an activity in which my father was trying to be helpful became disruptive. He'd prepare enough food for ten people. He'd wake up my mom for breakfast when all she wanted to do was sleep. He'd use all the week's groceries in one fell swoop—that sort of thing.

My dad's out-of-the-box approach to life made him a controversial figure at the university. Since he hated all authority, he saw institutions as places where people's minds were limited by rules. He demanded, instead, the right to teach his students in the best way he knew how. Because literature was sacred to him, he was willing to fight fanatically, no matter how minor the point. As my mom said, "Ken Hughes just can't leave anything alone." He was always writing to the president of the university about one issue or another—each cause a fight to the death. He had friends willing to support him on occasion, so he must have been right at least part of the time. Poignantly, during my dad's last days, when he could barely speak, he would take old letters out from an enormous stack of papers and show them to us. He clearly felt vindicated, but only he knew why. Despite the downside to my father's obsessions, I value the fact that he thought critically and against the grain. He instilled those qualities in me, which is why I never settle for something I believe is wrong or let anyone push my friends or me around.

4

REBEL

When I was in grade three, I forged a note from my mom. It said, "I give my daughter permission to buy twenty-five Benson & Hedges Deluxe Ultra Lights." I handed it to the IGA clerk, along with a sweaty handful of dimes, nickels, and pennies, then held my breath to see if she would accept it. She did.

It was also in grade three that I started stealing. I was strong, and my sister, Dodie, was mean. We were a deadly combo, although it wasn't long before she rocketed off into her own orbit. Dodie would stroll out of Zellers with curling irons, piles of makeup, and other stuff, but the first time I tried a big heist, I got caught. My friend and I stood in front of the candy counter loading our pockets with gum and chocolates. We were pretty obvious. A security guard grabbed us in the parking lot. "You can't just walk out without paying."

When he made us empty our pockets in front of a Dumpster, I had the audacity to say, "I can't believe we got caught!" That was true. I was so used to seeing my dad get away with whatever he wanted that I thought this was how the world worked. Though that attitude would get me into trouble, in retrospect I think it also gave me the confidence and the capacity and the drive to achieve goals as an adult that otherwise might have seemed out of reach. Still, all that was a long way off. At the moment, I was just a kid caught sticky-handed by a guy in a uniform. When the store officials called my parents, I feared the Belt. All I remember was my father raving, "No daughter of mine is a thief!"

That must have made some impression, because I didn't steal from stores again. Later, my friends and I did steal from our parents—booze and cigarettes, which I began smoking regularly in grade six. I also stole from my grandmother and was caught once again and felt bad once again. That still didn't stop me from stealing when I could. I lacked a strong moral background and a firm grasp on what was right and wrong. I also remember my dad yelling, "No child of mine will ever go to a bloody church!"

Our Elmwood neighbourhood was a cross-section of humanity. I grew up with friends from Chile, Jamaica, India, Pakistan, the Philippines, and China, along with many First Nations kids. My dad used to say, "Clara, never put anyone below you, and never put anyone above you. There are good and bad people—you can't deceive yourself into thinking otherwise—but this has nothing to do with race or income."

I liked the fact that Elmwood gave me a chance to experience the broadness of life, but it was also a rough, hardscrabble neighbourhood where you could get into all the trouble you wanted, and then some.

After my dad moved into his own apartment, he gave my mom the house, along with the task of bringing up Dodie and me. At forty-six, my mom learned to drive. She also took a nine-to-five job as a secretary at city hall. She held things together as best she could, but after my sister and I shed my father's strict expectations, we grew up fast. Too fast. When my mom tried to spank us with a spoon, we just laughed. It was a mean thing to do, and I felt terrible afterward, but Dodie didn't seem affected at all.

According to my mom, Dodie always liked to stay away from the house, whereas I liked to have friends over. When something made Dodie angry, she walked out, as my father had done. She was a puzzle to me, as well as to the rest of our family. Once, as a little kid, after she cut herself on glass at the beach, she started laughing maniacally instead of crying. I also remember her kicking one of my friends so hard that she almost broke the girl's leg. When my mom told a doctor she thought Dodie seemed hyperactive, he said, "Oh, don't worry. Everything will be fine."

But it never was. Though both my sister and I were messed up by our dysfunctional family, Dodie was soon out of control. By thirteen, she was into drugs and hanging around with some pretty rough people. She also became abusive to our mom, taking the role vacated by our dad. I remember, once, writing down every swear word she yelled at Mom, fascinated but horrified. I filled an eight-and-a-half-by-eleven sheet of paper, then turned it over and filled half of the other side before Dodie stormed out of the house. I knew this was wrong, but I didn't know what to do about it, or even if I wanted to do something about it. With Dodie deflecting my mom's attention, I could do anything I wanted. Later, my mom said, "Dodie was always in my face, whereas you found easier ways to get what you wanted."

When Mom began to fear for Dodie's survival, she resorted to tough love. After finding drugs in Dodie's room, she called the police. Suddenly, in the middle of the night, I heard strange, heavy footsteps stomping through the darkness of our house. These were followed by some awful howling from my sister's room. After that—and now from the street—I heard the metallic *thwump* of a car door closing. Then, silence.

So began my sister's frightening, decades-long journey of struggle. Though she moved in with my dad for a while, she never returned to our Elmwood house, where my mother still lives. Now that I understand my own emotional problems, I can better appreciate the factors behind my sister's struggle. Despite periods of estrangement, Dodie remains a vital part of me.

Back in Elmwood in 1985, Dodie was still the older sister I looked up to. When I was thirteen—Dodie's age when she moved out—I drank for the first time. Extra Old Stock because it was the beer with the highest alcoholic content. The bottle was heavy, and the booze syrupy and strong, but it wasn't the taste I was after, it was the fast fix. I chugged about eleven beers, probably in record time, and ate a bag of ketchup chips. After that, I phoned my mom, waking her to tell her I was staying all night at a friend's house. I didn't want her to see me drunk.

Mom gave me one of her typically patient responses, "Okay, dear, I'll see you in the morning."

I fell asleep, then barfed all over myself and my friend's bathroom floor. If I'd been on my back, I might have choked to death. I had no sense of consequences. Even after that, I kept right on drinking.

At thirteen, and already five-foot-nine, I could pass as eighteen, especially wearing lots of makeup. That meant I was able to buy beer using a fake ID, which a guy at school made in his drafting class. After I lent it to a friend, she got caught at a bar. Because my name was on it, the vice squad called my mom, then interrogated me. They asked where I got the ID, which was of good quality. I told them it was from an Indian downtown, because I knew that was vague enough and plausible enough that no one would be blamed.

From twelve to fourteen, I was enthralled with heavy metal bands like Judas Priest, Iron Maiden, and Mötley Crüe. I wore their T-shirts, along with a Harley-Davidson hoodie. I was a headbanger, violently whipping my head back and forth, with no sense of whether the music was good or bad. I was still trying to be like my sister, whom I scarcely knew anymore.

When I was around fifteen, my music tastes shifted to British new wave and electronic bands like Depeche Mode, and I began drinking big time. It was usually hard liquor, especially vodka straight from the bottle. The goal was always to get plastered. I was a happy drunk and fun to be around, until I reached the point of no return and puked all over myself or passed out under lampposts. Yes, I actually did that. I had alcohol poisoning so many times, without going to a hospital, that hard liquor seems like paint thinner to me now, so I usually avoid it. Back then, I was just socializing, doing what everyone else was doing, without understanding that putting these substances into my body could have serious long-term repercussions. On a deeper level, I believe that the alcohol and the drugs were my way of pushing down all the things inside me that I couldn't face—my confusion, my sense of failure, my self-hatred, my inability to fix my family.

At first, my drinking buddies were friends from school and the neighbourhood, but then I began partying with gangs who hung out downtown. We'd go into parking garage stairwells to get hammered, sitting on the concrete floor, sharing vodka or whatever anyone had. It was ugly drinking, and we'd buy weed indiscriminately. We didn't care from whom. Still, I smoked only occasionally, because I hallucinate easily, hearing and seeing things that grow and shrink. That made me feel out of control in a way I didn't like.

After we were completely shit-faced, the bunch of us would take a bus to a teenagers' nightclub called Changes, where drinking wasn't allowed. Why they let us in, I'll never know.

During this period, I was switching friends all the time, going from group to group. I was also a fashion chameleon, rotating my style in about six-month phases to blend in with everyone else. If the other girls sported tight jeans, red lipstick, and black eyeshadow, that became my uniform. If they wore their hair curly or feathered back, so did I. At one point, I shaved half my head, leaving my hair shoulder-length on the other half. I was being rebellious, but without any individuality—a follower rather than a leader. I never saw myself as attractive. I had different boyfriends, none of whom lasted. I would be drawn to someone because I imagined being with him would make me feel the way I wanted to feel about myself. Since that never happened, I would get bored, decide he was the wrong guy, and want out.

When I was an adolescent, my mom had given me a book about menstruation and sex, suggesting that we look at it together. No way! Around thirteen, I started sleeping around, which was as normal for my group as the drinking. I didn't know what I was doing—young, drunken fumbling, random and detached from any sense of reality. The sex was never memorable, or connected with love. Sex as a loving experience happened for me only much later in my life.

A lot of elite athletes never had much of a life before they began competing, but I'd already had several. While the memories aren't great, they're mine, and probably more normal than those of the kid who is institutionalized early into competitive sport. For all my problems, I'm grateful that I never was that senior athlete who realized she'd done nothing but train all of her life. I knew how it felt to drink and party and do drugs, so after I became good at sports, I didn't need to find out what I'd missed, though I did regress when depression hit me later. Even as an adult, I didn't know for a long time who I was, but I always felt I would somehow be able to channel my energy toward something positive, and I still do.

Given the intensity of my social life, Elmwood High School was very much an afterthought. If I didn't feel like attending, I didn't, and to my knowledge, no principal or vice-principal ever called home. I didn't like any of the subjects I had to study, especially math and science, and if I didn't like a teacher, that teacher knew it. I remember telling one in junior high to fuck off.

I did enjoy writing and art, and I especially liked my art teacher, Mr. Stevens. He always saw the best in us, not only encouraging our creativity but also urging us to take better care of ourselves by not smoking or doing drugs. Though that didn't make much impression on me, his belief in every one of us did. I could see that he was a good person.

Our school didn't offer much in the way of seriously competitive sports. I played volleyball, then signed up for a year of track and field. I never trained. I was never the star. I had no dreams of grand achievement, and didn't care as much as the other kids about winning. In grade eleven, I had only 60 percent in phys ed.

After my parents separated, they took another eighteen years to decide to divorce. My dad would often come to our Elmwood house, usually riding his bike. My mom would take him grocery shopping, basically acting as his taxi driver. Sometimes he was nice to her, but often he wasn't. My mother was—and is—a really good person, a peacemaker. As the middle child in a broken family with an alcoholic father, she was always trying to make things okay for everybody else. Those were the coping skills—and, I suppose, the enabling skills—that she brought to our family.

My father was a blamer. Everything that went wrong, or that he didn't like, was someone else's fault—my sister's, my grandmother's, my mother's. Mostly my mother's. It was always: "Your mother did this, your mother did that, your mother—your mother—your mother . . ."

Despite the overwhelming evidence that my dad was primarily responsible for the dysfunction in our family, I took his side. I blamed my mother as well. So did my sister. Mom was such an easy target. I didn't see her as human. I didn't see her struggle. I didn't see her courage. I didn't feel sorry for her—perhaps I didn't dare. That would mean doing something about what was going on when I didn't know how. Perhaps I needed all my energy to survive.

At events like Christmas, our broken family would gather, pretending we were normal. Sometimes it was okay, but most of the time my father would blow up, then storm out of the house. Once, after I had left home and returned as a visitor, I beat him to it by leaving on Christmas Eve.

As a kid, I would visit my dad in his apartment, and since he had abdicated all responsibility for my sister and me, it was fun. I could eat anything I wanted now that he wasn't cooking. I could laugh and be noisy and ignore his idea of how children should behave. He more or less supported my contemptuous attitude toward school, because he said grades and report cards put students in boxes, limiting them rather than inspiring them.

I still saw my father through rose-coloured glasses, even though he was drinking all the time. As I watched him pass out, while waiting for my mom to take me home, I would sometimes wonder: *Dad, why do you have to keep doing that? Why can't we just be together and talk and be happy?* I never understood what being an alcoholic meant, and I didn't connect what my friends and I were doing with what he did.

Learning how to block out, compartmentalize, and deny what was going on no doubt helped me become an Olympic athlete. It also meant I was an athlete with a shitload of baggage.

5

DREAM INTERRUPTED

When I was a little kid, my dad made a backyard rink—just a carpet-sized patch of ice around our walnut tree. It was pretty low-tech, created with a hose, but good enough for me. I was a natural skater. I played ringette from age six to sixteen, and hockey for one year when I was twelve—the only girl in the club league. My position was right defence, but after I was moved to forward for one game, I scored three times for a hat trick.

In high school, I won a speed-skating competition at the Winnipeg Arena, wearing stubby old hockey skates that were great for pivoting but not for wonderful, forward-gliding strokes. For that you needed straighter, sharper long blades. I enjoyed going to the rink, but it wasn't until one February day when I was sixteen that I had a transformative experience that would change skating from kids' stuff into a dream I had to achieve.

I was sitting in our living room, feeling bored and flipping through the channels, when I happened upon coverage of the 1988 Olympics in Calgary. Suddenly, I found myself staring at gold-medal speed skater Gaétan Boucher as he prepared to take what would be his last shot at the podium in the men's 1500 metres. I watched, mesmerized, as he glided effortlessly, his body beautifully coordinated, his blades barely touching the ice, executing moves that must have taken him a lifetime to learn, doing what he obviously loved.

I thought: *I want to do that.* The fact that this was happening just two provinces away made my dream more possible, allowing me to be more emphatic: *I am going to do that!* It was a heart-stopping, life-affirming moment. I just *knew,* and it wasn't as if I was captured by a scene of triumph, because Gaétan finished ninth in that race.

The next day, I said to my mom, "I want to speed-skate in the Olympics."

Mom wasted no time in calling the Winnipeg Speed Skating Club. She found they were holding a training camp in the spring. Peter Williamson, Manitoba's provincial coach and a member of Canada's 1968 Olympic team, was conducting it. I was accepted, and Peter became my coach.

I started speed skating in my hockey skates, and thought I was pretty good, until I saw the others, so smooth and fast, gliding on their long blades. I rented a pair from the Speed Skating Club. They were ancient, with worn-out boots providing little support, resulting in painful ankles. It took a while before I managed fluidity on those long blades, yet I felt like a champ, guided by that vision I had seen on TV.

I bought my first pair of skates when I was seventeen—new to me, but second-hand. They were Viking speed skates, the kind used by the best skaters in the world, and cost $800, which I raised by selling my beat-up car for $700. The shiny black boots, with cream-coloured leather trim, fit my feet like tight leather gloves, while the seventeen-inch blades, separated by mirror-finished cups, gleamed like pure silver. They were still torturous to wear, because my feet hadn't toughened up, but I didn't care.

Peter Williamson was larger than life, a wonderful human being, a leader who demanded our best but who was always ready to break tension with a laugh. It was Peter who first inspired me to channel my abundant negative energy into something positive. Without him, my history in sports never would have happened. He had us training on bikes and roller skates, as well as on the ice, working harder than I had thought possible. I loved it. Peter also encouraged me to cut down on my smoking and drinking as part of my dedication to the sport. His keenness for integrating education with athletics even resulted in my returning to school, after months of hooky, to convert F's into A's.

At first, I wanted only to sprint because that meant I didn't have to train as much. Peter was disappointed that I wouldn't commit to distances, but I dreaded the exhaustion and the pain, which is ironic since endurance became my hallmark.

For the first time, I was surrounded by athletes who were driven to skate their very best, instead of by lost souls drinking their lives away. I had goals beyond getting wasted. I was plugged into something larger than me, I was evolving as a person and learning the meaning of self-respect. Sport provided me with a value system and a moral base that I had lacked. I wanted to be good for Peter, and that year—1989—I won silver at the National Championships in Calgary for the 800-metre, mass-start event. Though I knew this wasn't the Olympics, I felt pumped. My reward was earning Peter's praise and knowing I deserved it.

Unfortunately, this excitement proved short-lived. Peter Williamson was drafted for a sports job in Ottawa, leaving me devastated. I found myself skating around and around on my long silver blades, without a team, without goals or focus.

My vision of floating over the ice without seeming to touch it had become a dream interrupted . . .

THE BIKE
1990–2000

6

ESCAPE

When I was six, I received my first bike. It was small, orange, and—most important—didn't have training wheels. The grown-ups said, "You'll have to learn to ride that." I just hopped on, and off I went. It was easy. When I was around twelve, I bought a ridiculous white-and-pink BMX racing bike. I remember doing a wheelie down the lane, landing on my ass, and laughing, because I figured next time I'd get it right.

I was a natural rider.

What I didn't know was that road racing would dominate my life for the next two decades, and, yes, I would land on my ass and worse many more times.

After Peter Williamson left for Ottawa, I was eighteen, at loose ends, and eager for a new challenge. Mirek Mazur, the Manitoba cycling coach, had seen me skate and wanted me to try out for his team. The 1990 Western Canada Summer Games were to be held in Winnipeg, so the Manitoba government had established a grant to recruit more women into cycling. I was invited to attend a training camp in the Black Hills of South Dakota.

Riding back home in the team van, Mirek singled me out. At thirty, he was good-looking, very fit, with short blond hair and intense blue eyes that he fixed on me. He had observed that I was the girl able to stay at the pace set by the guys the longest, so now he wanted me to drop speed skating for cycling.

"I can make you a world champion," he told me. "If you do what I say, you could win the women's Tour de France. How would you like to wear the yellow jersey?"

Before the South Dakota camp, I hadn't even known cycling was a sport. When I'd seen young people wandering around Winnipeg in team jerseys, I'd thought they'd probably bought them at the same store, like members of a glee club. Mirek exuded a certain power though. When he looked at me, with an unapologetic intensity, he triggered a devotion to sport, to competition, that had lain dormant inside me. His goal was to build his riders into impossibly committed and driven athletes, using stern, unforgiving, Eastern Bloc methods. Because he was a native of Poland, coaching was a vocation that he pushed to extremes, though I didn't know that at the time.

For better or for worse, Mirek changed my life. After graduating from high school, I committed myself to the bike. Mirek made me want to be good, very good. As a speed skater, I had never been driven to push myself in the way Mirek now demanded. Mirek made me a more complete athlete, certainly one more focused on endurance. Skating had given me the dream, but cycling would teach me the discipline.

I trained relentlessly—*we* trained relentlessly, six of us, a great group of young women who did everything together. We were driven by thoughts of the 1990 Western Games—a drive that came with a big payoff.

The first shock to our competitors came when our team won gold in the Western Games team time trial. For this race, the four-person teams start a couple of minutes apart, with the winning team being the one to complete the course the fastest. Since a team is allowed to drop one member, it receives its time after the third member crosses the finish line. For the best result, team members must work closely together, one behind the other, with the lead rider pushing into the wind, while the others "draft" in the slipstream, where there's less work to do. After thirty seconds or a minute, the lead rider drops back, and the second rider takes the lead, and so on. It's as if the team is a single rider, with eight wheels racing in unison to the finish line.

I won my second Western Games gold in individual pursuit. For this, two cyclists begin the 3-kilometre race from a standing start on opposite sides of a velodrome. When the gun goes off, so do the cyclists, pursuing each other on the steeply banked oval track, trying to lap each other, or at least to finish in the fastest time. Though cyclists are urged to pace themselves so they have energy to end the race, I was so ridiculously fit that I could pedal all-out, with my first and last laps at about the same speed.

I won my third Western Games gold for the points race. Competitors start at the same time, each balanced with one hand on a support. When the gun goes off, each cyclist pushes away, then starts pedalling around the velodrome. Since the bike has a fixed gear and no brakes, there is no stopping, in what is a long race with many laps. Points are awarded for sprints within the race and for lapping the main field. The winner is the cyclist who scores the most points—which I did.

I won a fourth gold for a 1-kilometre race on the track, and a silver medal for a criterium road race.

The success of our unheralded prairie team came as a big surprise. I remember riding through downtown Winnipeg with people leaning out of their cars to yell: "Go, Team Manitoba!" It was the first time I felt special. We'd won something for our city, *my* city. It made me want to lose myself in riding, burning like I'd never burned before.

This determination paid off once again at the 1990 National Championships, where I won three gold medals in the track competition.

Despite having given up skating, I received a grant from the Manitoba government to buy new skates, so it seemed silly not to use them. I competed in the Canadian Cup Junior Champion selection races in Regina, where I won the 3000 metres after not having skated for a year. That qualified me for the Junior Worlds, but I declined to go, preferring to focus on cycling.

I'd always been a big kid who played for the fun of it, and now, with the drive Mirek had instilled in me, my life was coming together. I even quit smoking so I could put my head and heart completely into my new sport.

In 1991, Mirek was recruited by Ontario as their provincial cycling coach. After losing Peter Williamson to a similar promotion, I knew how it felt to be a single athlete, aimlessly struggling against a strong headwind, and I didn't want that happening again. When Mirek invited me to move to Ontario with him, I quickly agreed. At nineteen, I was an adult in charge of my life, unlike many athletes who were managed by their parents. In any event, both my parents were supportive. As my father graphically put it, "Get out of this hellhole and don't come back. You'll be dragged down in this mess and never come out."

Though he was describing his own life, my rebellious history made it a warning worth heeding.

Mirek had arrived at a pivotal time. All of my coaches became father figures to me, filling a vacuum in my life. Even when my dad had been physically present, he had never provided me with the positive reinforcement that I received from winning. Mirek gave me structure and clear goals. I wanted to be good for someone, and that someone was Mirek. No matter how bad our relationship would become, I felt freed from the fears and confusion and uncertainties that had kept me, as a child, hiding in a closet, and then drinking myself stupid in stairwells. I wanted to outride all my demons, leaving all that darkness behind me. Even though, of course, I couldn't.

Mirek and his son were living in a house outside of Hamilton, and another female cyclist and I moved in as well. Mirek's wife, Eva, remained in Winnipeg finishing her university degree in pharmacology.

I was being partially funded by Sport Canada's "carding" program, which gave assistance to qualifying athletes. For me, that meant about $650 a month to start. Big Dodie had generously bought me my first road bike—a white, basic-level Cannondale that probably cost about $700. For my second bike, I paid around $1500. After that, my bikes were supplied by sponsors, beginning with the Specialized-Pedal Racing Team.

The rest of my income came from winning criterium races, held across Ontario. Usually they were 1.0- to 1.5-kilometre loops, ridden thirty to fifty times on roads in and around cities and towns. The loops were closed to traffic, with a lead car and a follow car and police support. Since criterium races were fast-paced, with crowds of cyclists taking corners at the same time, they could be dangerous.

What attracted me were the purses. If I could win $350 for a forty-five-minute race, then, *Wow, why wouldn't I?* I certainly didn't want to ask Mom or Big Dodie or my dad for money, though their support was always there.

When Mirek and I were on the road, we roomed together for budgetary reasons. There was nothing shady about that, no boundaries were ever crossed, but it was depressing. We spent months training in places like Pine Valley, a nothing village in California, where I had no friends, felt isolated, and was in a state of exhaustion the whole time.

Mirek refused to allow his athletes to submit to frailty or show any kind of vulnerability. We trained eleven months a year, with almost no days off. We lived cycling—wall to wall, day to day, hour to hour. It was all Mirek all the time.

If you watch really good riders, you'll see their pedalling has a beautiful fluidity, like a well-oiled sewing machine. I never had that grace, except to some degree in my last years, when I worked with a different coach who deliberately set about to change my style. Mirek's methods for turning me into a champion—a world champion—were crude: massive amounts of training, in which I cycled really big gears, using my strength instead of leg speed. I would grind out the same intervals, day after day. I'd do 4×10 minutes, which meant cycling at time-trial pace for ten minutes, repeated four times, with four minutes' rest in between. Or maybe 10×1 kilometre, cycling 1 kilometre ten times with little rests after each one. Because my taste of winning—of achieving—was still sweet, I steeled myself against the rigours of training. I convinced myself that what Mirek required of me wasn't so bad, and since I was naturally strong, I could handle the huge gears. For a while, I could, but it did catch up to me. In 1993, I had acute tendinitis, and in 1994, I had hip problems.

Canadian cyclist Michael Barry, who sometimes worked with Mirek, later would tell me: "Mirek suffocated part of who you were. I remember seeing you at one race in the middle of summer, and it was stinking hot. We were all trying to get cool so as not to melt before the race, but you were in a parking lot, under the awning of a mechanics' stall, doing your intervals because Mirek said you should."

Mirek set unrealistic goals, and—what was worse for me—he believed in negative motivation, his alpha-male way of dealing with any situation. He was always making fun of me for being fat. During some training camps, he would require me to walk one or two hours before breakfast to cut down on my appetite. Then his contemptuous look and tone made me feel like a glutton when I ate the little I allowed myself to eat.

Feeling starved and empty of all but self-loathing, I trained harder at first, but soon enough, I'd head down to the nearest 7-Eleven to stand at the cooler in my flip-flops and shorts, staring through the smudged glass behind which they kept the Eskimo Pies and other treats. I'd sink my hands into the cooler, then yank out the ice cream—an elite athlete, in the best shape of her life, tearing open the wrapping with frantic fingers or teeth, then forcing the chocolate or the wafer or the caramel into the enormous emotional void that racing was creating.

During one training camp, I met a female athlete who ate only saltine crackers, and I wanted to be just like her. I was far stronger, but all I could think about was her ability to exist on crackers. When a friend of mine saw another racer, always held up as an example of fitness and beauty, he exclaimed, "My god, Clara, she's practically anorexic." He was right. After she left racing, she acknowledged that she'd quit partly because of the stress of dieting and her obsession with weighing herself.

A lot of cyclists, male as well as female, have eating disorders because of the brutality of the sport, along with the conflict of food for strength versus lightness for speed. I would fill page after page with my calorie counts, wanting to stay below 800. Then, I would hide food and binge, creating a loop of self-hatred and guilt, causing me to eat more. I wanted to be light and small and unburdened, like those athletes sick with anorexia. Instead, I felt like I was carrying around an enormous heaviness, both physically and emotionally.

My honeymoon with cycling as a confidence builder proved short. In retrospect, I believe I was in a state of subclinical depression for about seven years. I was already too hard on myself, because of my traumatic childhood, and Mirek's methods exacerbated those deep-seated insecurities.

Everyone could see what was happening to me psychologically.

Everyone but me. I started to believe that I could never be any good without Mirek. I had no sense of self-worth. If I had berated other people the way I berated myself, I wouldn't have had a single friend.

The first time I rebelled against Mirek was at the 1991 Pan American Games in Havana, Cuba. That was also the first international competition in which I represented Canada. Mirek was coach of the national men's team, but I was with the women's team under a different coach. Though I was expected to train with Mirek as well, he seemed threatened by the coaching competition. Apparently his way of dealing with that was to be meaner to me than usual.

Mirek was always pushing, pushing, pushing. Eventually I told him, "Fuck off!" After that, we stopped communicating.

Unfortunately, the training style of the women's coach didn't suit me. Besides, I was nineteen years old, at my first international competition, wearing Canada's team jersey, and I thought I should at least be enjoying myself.

I was wrong. I lost discipline. I barely ate, except for ice cream, three times a day. I knew nothing about nutrition—nobody was talking about energy foods back then—and I grew weak. Instead of basking in the excitement and feeling great about the opportunity, I was constantly brooding. *I'm expected to win for a coach I hate?*

My Pan Am experience taught me a lesson that I'd prefer to have learned in a more positive way. Ever after, in high-level competition, I would remind myself: *You aren't here to eat ice cream, to have fun, or to indulge yourself, which are all things you can do for the rest of your life. Ignore others. Keep your focus. Run your own race.*

The Canadian women's team, which included me, captured bronze in the team time trial. In the individual pursuit, I pulled my foot out of the pedal at the start, forcing me to chase from behind. I did win silver, but I should have won gold.

Here's the truth, though: There was no depth in the field that year in Cuba. In the cycling hierarchy, the Olympics are at the top, with the World Championships next, then the Commonwealth Games, and then the Pan Ams. Because of conflicting dates, the top-level competitors were at the World Championships, so this was a second-class race.

Adding to my depression was my growing realization that the Cuban people were starving outside the gates, while those of us in the Athletes' Village could stuff ourselves with anything we wanted. Since the collapse of the Soviet Union, most Cuban lives were no longer sustainable. Before I left for home, I gave all of my Team Canada clothes to the hotel doorman, who reciprocated with the gift of a little pin. This was the first time I felt connected to our host nation. It was a small gesture, but it taught me another valuable lesson—the importance of reaching out, or at least trying to.

Back in Canada, a tragic shock awaited me. I discovered that my first coach, Peter Williamson, had died, age forty-four, of an aneurysm, leaving his wife, Lori, and his four children. It hit me hard. Ever afterward, when I won some honour, I felt sad that Peter would never know one of his athletes had achieved international success, thanks to his profound influence coming when it was most needed.

I tried to push down all this grief, along with a black churn of other emotions, guaranteeing that it was only a matter of time before I would break. Cycling—the training, the culture, the lifestyle—fed my negativity and despair. Sadly, it's a sport that made me feel like garbage even when I won.

I was rotting from the inside.

7

HITTING THE ROAD—HARD!

I was back training with Mirek, as I'm sure he knew I would be. I expected fallout from both my attitude and subpar performance in Cuba, and I got it. During the buildup to the 1992 Olympics in Barcelona, Mirek leaned on me even harder, complaining sarcastically when I took a day off: "Oh, so you need a rest, do you, Clara?"

In 1991, I won three gold medals at the National Championships in Calgary, but that was because Canada's two best racers were still at the World Championships. I believed that I had a chance to beat at least one of them, but now I would never know.

Since the National Speed Skating Championships were also held in Calgary that year, I competed in those as well, setting a Junior Canadian record.

After qualifying for the 1992 Olympic cycling trials on the track, I went to Germany to train for the first time with Canada's sprint team and the men's endurance squad. Sprinting is all about speed, and these athletes were tightly wound machines. We were staying at a hotel, near the town of Büttgen, with a really good restaurant. The sprinters seemed able to eat whatever they wanted, especially a lot of protein. I consumed mounds of protein right along with them, also piling on the pasta, the cream sauce, the bread, and the desserts. I had no idea you could put on ten pounds in three weeks, which is what I did. Then, before I raced in a World Cup event in Stuttgart, I crashed into a post on the bike path, leaving me bruised and beaten. It was not a good trip.

On my return to Canada, ten days before the Olympic track trials, Mirek exclaimed in shock, "My god, what happened to you?"

"What do you mean?"

"Look at you, you're fat!"

"What are you talking about?"

At the Olympic track trials, I was as slow as a turtle. I came in third. Not so bad? Except only three women were competing. I was dead last.

Mirek said, "You blew it for track. Why don't you try the road race trials?"

In road racing, performance is based on a power-to-weight ratio. Since Peter Williamson, my skating coach, had also told me my strength lay in endurance, I thought maybe Mirek was right.

The road race trials were in Dundas, Ontario, that year. I didn't make the Olympic team, but I did well enough to be invited to compete in the Ore-Ida Women's Challenge, an Idaho stage race attracting the world's best cyclists.

A stage race consists of several road races, time trials, and circuit races, run consecutively day after day, with everyone starting at the same time. Awards are given for winning individual stages, and the overall winner is the person or team that completes all the stages in the fastest cumulative time.

In 1992, the Ore-Ida Women's Challenge was considered so gruelling that the Union Cycliste Internationale, the sport's governing board, refused to sanction it. They stated their reasons in a 1990 memorandum: "excessive number of stages" over "excessive individual stage distances" with "excessive climbing" for an "excessive duration," often resulting in an excessive number of crashes.

To attract competitors, the Ore-Ida Challenge offered one of the most lucrative purses in women's cycling—around $25,000 when I entered, building up to $125,000 over the next decade.

A stage road race, with its dozens of competitors, requires its own special strategy. Most riders bunch together in a pack or peloton because drafting, or riding in someone's slipstream, can reduce the effort of pedalling by as much as 40 percent. At some point in the race, a group of riders might break from the group to gain a significant lead. Typically, this is a team tactic, with members working together to save the energy of their sprinter, who "sits" in the draft until making a final dash to the finish line, winning for herself and her team.

Though I was with the National B Team at the 1992 Ore-Ida, we had no plan beyond competing to survive and to gain experience. Therefore, I was devising my own strategy, kilometre by kilometre, for fourteen days. Temperatures soared to 90°F (32°C). We cycled through sagebrush, sometimes fighting fierce headwinds, with severe climbs through mountain passes. Since the peloton was travelling at 40 to 50 kilometres per hour, with dozens of wheels only inches apart, an exhausted rider, failing to hold her line, might bring down several others. A pothole might throw a cyclist, a tire might blow—creating more pile-ups, more twisted bikes, more broken bones.

It was while spending fourteen days with these endurance athletes that I learned the fine points of eating for my sport. Though Mirek had already heightened my self-consciousness about my weight, these women took dieting to a whole new level. I'd be enjoying a salad when someone would say, "Um, you know that has dressing on it, don't you?" I'd be eating a piece of bread when someone would say, "You know if you eat the middle part it will expand in your stomach, right?" Raw veggies? "Well, not too many because of water retention." Soup? "Too much salt." Desserts? I knew enough not to ask.

At first, I'd believed that cyclists and support staff ate at separate tables because of some sort of elitist division. Then I noticed that the staff would be devouring steaks and french fries while the athletes, with dark circles under their eyes, were huddled around their undressed salads and boiled vegetables. During one stage race at the end of the season, I saw a rider who was so thin and sinewy I swore I saw her veins through her shorts.

Though I made the front of the peloton only once during the 1992 Ore-Ida, I finished the final time trial in the top twenty—quite an accomplishment for a rookie. The Ore-Ida was ridiculously difficult, but I loved it.

By the end of 1992, I had won my first national road race championship and title, and I had finished top ten in my first European stage race,
the Tour of the Economic Community.

I was hooked on road racing!

In 1993, I signed my first professional racing contract—with Team
Kahlúa Cycling. I was promised $7000 but received only $3500. The
team folded because of mismanagement. I never cared about the money,
but the betrayal disappointed me.

That first year of racing as a pro, I crashed in every stage race. In
Arizona, during La Vuelta de Bisbee, I remember being slammed from
the left by another rider on a descent with 3 kilometres left in the race. I
smashed into the guardrail at about 70 kilometres per hour and tumbled
to the ground, then somehow managed to stand. My front wheel was
ripped in half, and I had road rash across my whole back. As I stumbled
away, a mechanic from a support vehicle caught up to me. He replaced
my front wheel, and I climbed back on my bike, then hammered to the
finish line.

That same year, I was sitting in second place overall in the Tour
de l'Aude Cycliste Féminin, which was basically the women's version
of the Tour de France, when I was caught in another nasty crash.
Once again, my wheel was destroyed, and I wasted precious minutes
waiting for a support vehicle to catch up to replace it. I managed to
grind my way back to the peloton that day, and then, later in the
tour, up the historic L'Alpe d'Huez in the Rhône-Alpes, with its stiff
13.8-kilometre climb and twenty-one hairpin bends. I finished a respectable nineteenth overall. Instead of a yellow jersey, my souvenir
was a huge scar on my shoulder.

You learn how to crash right by crashing a lot. You learn the skill of
riding over ditches and even people. Once, I rode over someone's arm
as if it were a road bump. You learn to skirt crashes instead of reacting
to them.

When you do go down, the first thing you're aware of is the sound—
that terrible scraping of metal across pavement, and the screaming that

happens before you hit the ground. Then, it's the terrible abrasive shock of flesh connecting with pavement. If others go down, you hope none of them are your teammates. You check to see if you can move: *Is anything broken?* Then: *Where's my bike? Can I get back on?* Though it's terrible to leave one of your teammates lying injured, that's what we're trained to do.

Crashes are an integral part of cycling. My friend Michael Barry has said, "During the Tour de France, there are sometimes thirty injuries in one day, and, sometimes, this happens four, five, six days in a row. If that happened in a factory, it would be shut down, but because it's sport, we somehow tolerate it."

My friend Dede Demet remembered a race in which a bunch of students poured oil on the road around a bend because they thought it would be cool to watch a crash. "That time, I shattered my cheekbone," she said.

Racing in Europe, where cycling was taken more seriously than in North America, taught me a great deal about the dark side of the sport.

I've competed in the Tour de l'Aude Cycliste Féminin four times. On two occasions, part of the race went up the L'Alpe d'Huez. Each of the hairpin turns is named for a male Tour de France rider who won one of its stages. The women's races on those same slopes went virtually unnoticed. There were marked differences between men's and women's cycling. Though practised at different levels, neither was immune to the use of performance-enhancing drugs.

Since I was pretty naïve, it took me time to catch on to what was happening all around me. I saw girls who couldn't climb hills to save their lives suddenly winning mountain stages. I remember one Lithuanian coach telling me, "If you want to compete with the Russians, you should pay fifty-thousand dollars for their doping program." Whether or not this might be true of the Russians, I realized then that doping was a serious concern.

Gradually, I began to notice some racers had locked compartments in their bags. I saw a team with a centrifuge machine for testing vials of their blood for hemoglobin levels—the concentration of red blood cells. At first, I thought they were being vigilant about their diets and their training routine, and I was, like, *Wow, what a cool machine!* They were so fit, I began to feel like a slacker.

Eventually, I learned there was a process of taking synthetic erythropoietin, or EPO. This is the chemical form of a hormone naturally produced by the kidneys to artificially stimulate production of red blood cells, increasing the efficiency with which oxygen is transported from the lungs into the muscles. If doses were timed far enough before competition, the doper could train significantly harder and longer, while eliminating all traces of synthetic EPO before race time. That began to change in 2000, when newer tests were developed that allowed authorities—and the world—to learn how rampant doping had become.

Another way to boost the number of red blood cells was through transfusions of one's own stored blood, or that of a compatible donor. As well, human growth hormones are used to increase muscle mass and power, and steroids like testosterone also stimulate muscle development and the kidneys' ability to produce natural EPO. In females, the side effects of taking these hormones include virilization, which is the development of facial hair and a deepening of the voice, increased aggression, mood swings, depression, irregular menstrual cycles, potential jaundice, and liver damage. I personally saw bodies transformed over a few weeks that caused me to wonder: *Is that still a girl?*

Stimulants like amphetamines, ephedrine, cocaine, and salbutamol aid weight loss and act on the brain to allow athletes to compete at higher levels for longer by reducing fatigue.

Doping among female cyclists wasn't nearly as prevalent as among male cyclists, where millions of dollars were at stake. When there's money and power, corruption follows. On any given day, you can read about greed and substance abuse in the church, state, and corporate sector. While sports heroes are often glorified, they reflect the common weaknesses of society. Some athletes surrounded themselves with the wrong people. Some couldn't resist the enormous pressures that allowed them no other choice except to quit.

Michael Barry, who rode with Lance Armstrong on the U.S. Postal Service Pro Cycling Team, was caught up in the same scandal as Lance. As he explained, "When I was doping, all I cared about was achieving victory at all costs, but it took me almost dying to see things in a different light. We lived in a bubble and were so focused on tomorrow that we couldn't appreciate what was happening while it was happening. We had no perspective. We had no idea who we were, what we were doing, or why."

To Mirek's credit, he used to say, "Riders who use EPO are fucking cheaters, and I'd sooner be caught dead than let one of my riders do drugs."

I personally never even considered doping, because I was a successful rider in a sport where I had a chance to win without drugs, though perhaps not all the time. I also associated drugs with a part of my life that I didn't wish to repeat. Sport had helped me escape a self-destructive culture—a fact that was reinforced by a horrible shock I received during a visit home to Winnipeg about this same time.

Dodie, who was twenty-three to my twenty-one, was living with my dad. When I first saw her, she was lying on a couch, on sick leave from work as a nurse's aide and looking terrible. I remember sitting beside her and asking, "How's everything?"

She couldn't answer. Instead, she just started crying. I didn't know what was wrong. Today, I understand that she was in a deep, clinical depression. A lot of nasty things had happened to her because of the drugs and her mental state. I was home from winning races, and even my asking about her life had hurt her. In her eyes, I was the gifted daughter, the successful one, the pride of Winnipeg. I didn't know what to do. She was my older sister, the defiant one who hadn't given a damn about anything. For a time, we had shared the same lifestyle. It terrified me to see how close I'd come to being the sister lying on that couch.

I was also traumatized to think that this might still be the fate I was running, riding, racing away from.

In 1994, I returned to Idaho for the Ore-Ida Challenge, renamed the PowerBar Women's Challenge. This time it was a six-stage race, held over five days, and this time I won it. It was an important victory, because I was competing as a guest with the Saturn Cycling Team, the best in the world, boosting my hopes that I would be invited to join them.

I was riding high. What a terrific season! Then, in late autumn of 1994, I was caught up in an athlete's worst nightmare. Pierre Hutsebaut, Canada's national team director, informed me that I had tested positive for the banned substance ephedrine at the World Championships in Sicily.

I was shattered.

I was also confused. I didn't even know what ephedrine was, and I couldn't imagine how it had found its way into my system. I began checking the labels on everything I had ingested, right down to my toothpaste. Though I never found any ephedrine, by then I knew it was a performance-enhancing stimulant. That was ironic, given that I had underperformed in the time trial—the race in which I'd tested positive—finishing only fourth after posting wins all season.

Pierre was certain that I had not intentionally taken any stimulant, as was our national team coach, Denis Roux. Since the penalty would be a three-month ban, which would fall over cycling's off-season, and since I had won no medal that would have to be returned, I was advised to keep quiet about the situation, which I did. Nevertheless, I felt gutted, as if I'd cheated, even though I hadn't. I still don't know if that was the right decision. That incident continued to eat at me throughout my career, contributing to my underlying sense of unworthiness.

In 1995, I did receive a contract to compete with Team Saturn, perhaps because I had remained silent. Our most important race that season was the Philadelphia Liberty Classic. As a one-day June event, it consisted of four laps creating a 57.6-mile circuit through Philadelphia. This included four climbs up the infamous Manayunk Wall, noted for its steep gradient and—in some places—worn cobblestones.

About 3 kilometres into the race, I went down in a huge crash. My hip was throbbing but my bike was okay, so I climbed back on, and even managed to catch up to the peloton. There was a sudden breakaway, which included two of my Saturn teammates. I told myself: *Just keep pedalling. Maybe you'll feel better sitting in the pack and spinning out the inflammation.*

The peloton caught the breakaway with less than 4 kilometres to go. A teammate, our fastest sprinter, asked me to attack, because she wasn't confident about doing the sprint. Though I was in terrible pain from what I thought was a broken hip, when a teammate asks you to do a job, you do it. No excuses.

With only 1 kilometre to go, I attacked on this big, sweeping round-about. Then, I just kept going. I ended up winning—what was then the most important single-day race of my life!

Joining Saturn was the awesome opportunity of which I had been dreaming. For my first year, I was paid $18,000, while learning from my teammates and winning with them. Since I was also subsidized by the government and collecting prize money, I felt well off for a young person who didn't own a car or anything else beyond what I needed to race. Because ours was a team effort, we pooled our winnings, then split them equally among everyone, including our staff. In a year, I might end up with about $25,000 in prize money.

At the 1995 Pan American Games in Argentina, I won a silver medal in the road race and a bronze in the time trial. While that may look good on paper, both "wins" were utter failures in terms of what I should have accomplished. I had been training with Canada's national team coach, Denis Roux, but ended up going back to Mirek. I still believed that Mirek, and only Mirek, made me any good. For five weeks, we did high-altitude training for the World Championship to be held in Colombia. Since the time trial was up a steep grade, everyone kept telling me that I wouldn't be able to do it because I was too big to go fast uphill. In fact, I won silver—my first and only World Championship medal in cycling.

After I had received my award, one coach sardonically said to me, "How much better do you think you would have done if you were five kilos lighter?"

That was enough to bring me down again.

Underlying all my success—all my reasons for feeling good—I was still carrying a dump truck load of negativity. Some of this was due to the pressure to perform, some of it was due to the emptiness and the loneliness that seemed an unshakeable part of me. My first feeling after winning was relief, followed by gratitude that I hadn't screwed up. Any sense of celebration was always short-lived. That was my father's legacy: *Okay, so you've won. So what? You were supposed to win, now let's move on.* My own inner voice would respond on cue: *Oh yeah. I guess I wasn't so good, after all.*

Like a junkie, I kept hoping my next big win would be the fix I needed. If not the Western Games, then maybe the Nationals. If not the Nationals, then maybe the Pan Ams. If not the Pan Ams, perhaps a World Championship. I had won medals at all of these levels of competition, and none had been sufficient. I had only one more "fix" left—the Olympics. Maybe if I won there, the success would magically transform me so I would actually know who I was and I'd feel really good about being that person.

And so, I set my sights on the 1996 Games in Atlanta.

8

ATLANTA OLYMPICS 1996

Though I had pre-qualified for Atlanta, I felt so unmotivated in my "drive" to the Games that I found it difficult even to finish a race. A great humiliation was my second-to-last place in the final stage of that year's Tour de l'Aude Cycliste Féminin.

I was desperate for a magical solution. I thought about all those skinny European cyclists who had beaten me. *What if I ate less—maybe nothing at all?* Starving made me feel empowered, even when my reserves sank so dangerously low I had to lean on a wall to keep from passing out.

Instead of feeling excited about competing for Canada, all I wanted was for the Olympics to be over. It didn't help when people reassured me by saying, "Oh, Clara, no matter what happens, you'll always have the memory of the Olympic experience." The more optimistic people added, "Maybe one day you *will* get to the podium."

What saved me from sinking into the tar pit of depression sucking at my feet was a small race in Collingwood, Ontario. It was a nothing race, more of a tune-up than a challenge, that I decided, on a whim, to enter. As I gloomily pedalled along, with about 10 kilometres to go, I reached a hill about the same time as Marianne Berglund, a sprinter from Sweden. I remember thinking: *Well, she's going to win.* All of a sudden, another voice inside my head challenged: *Why not attack and see what happens?* I started hammering away, lengthening my lead on Marianne and almost everyone else.

With about 5 kilometres to go, I had only one opponent left—Sue Palmer, the Canadian road race champion. I thought, *Well, Sue will beat me in the sprint.* Mirek was constantly telling me how useless I was as a sprinter, but now, in defiance, I again talked back: *No, I'll keep attacking.* And I did. Remarkably—or so it seemed at the time—I won that race. As a competition, it had meant little. However, psychologically, it meant everything. I'd managed to put Mirek's belittling voice out of my head, and from that day forward, I decided I would strive to win every single race, whether I was "suited" for it or not.

Before the Games, I trained with Mirek and the team in Pennsylvania, with me as the only woman. Mirek liked to point out how spoiled and privileged the American team was, with its nutritionists and slew of support staff. He thought our bare-bones living would make us stronger so that we would win more medals. In fairness, Mirek had no budget for anything better, and he made a lot happen, getting us to races and training camps, with very little funding.

Michael Barry, who was on the men's team, later confirmed what I was beginning to suspect, though: "Mirek was more demeaning to you than to the rest of us. He was very cold, very rough. One day, after he had flown home, I remember a bunch of us were out riding. Rather than do the assigned routine, we decided to turn right at a path where Mirek had told us to turn left. I remember you freaking out, insisting that we do what Mirek had told us to do. You were scared of him. I felt sorry for you. You were so alone and unhappy."

Though I now know Michael was right, I was still too insecure to believe I could succeed without Mirek.

Since Mirek wasn't invited to Atlanta as a coach, I flew to the Games by myself. No one was waiting to take me to the Athletes' Village, and I came close to mistakenly boarding a train to downtown Atlanta.

Even at the Athletes' Village, I found myself stranded, forlornly holding my bag, without any sense of what to do or where to go. When I approached the volunteers, they asked for my accreditation. I didn't have any. They contacted someone from the Canadian Olympic Committee, who sorted me out, but I was upset: *I'm competing for Canada, and this is the best anyone can do?*

After being assigned a room in a university dorm, I went for a gender test to prove I was female. Then I went back to my room, still feeling abandoned and alone: *Now what?* My connection to Mirek distanced me from the other riders on the Canadian team—an isolation I had not intended nor realized was happening. It was the little dark cloud that followed me around.

I went to the Village Plaza, where I found a concert in full force: the Foo Fighters. I watched other athletes whooping it up until my "too-much-ice-cream" experience at the Pan Am Games kicked in. I reminded myself: *Anyone can party. I can buy a ticket to a concert any time. I don't need this shit.* Everything was free—I could go somewhere and get a bonus bag, but why would I? The dining hall was enormous, with food piled everywhere. I walked by it all, sticking to my starvation diet.

I watched the Opening Ceremony on TV in the Athletes' Lounge, rather than marching into the stadium with the Canadian team, conserving my strength for my first race, which was in two days' time. Atlanta was the XXVI Olympiad. Over 10,000 participants from 197 nations were competing in 271 events; 307 of those were Canadian, with women outnumbering men for the first time, 154 to 153.

I didn't know anyone in the lounge. I felt as if I didn't belong there but hung in to see the lighting of the Olympic torch. When the person carrying the flame came into view, those around me let out a whoop.

I asked, "Who's that?"

"It's Muhammad Ali!"

"Who the fuck is Muhammad Ali?"

Having grown up in a non-sporting family, how was I to know?

I had only two days to train before my first event—the 104-kilometre road race. A couple of times I found myself eating with Eric Van den

Eynde, a national team coach, a Québécois originally from Belgium. I considered him irritating because he talked too much, telling stories when I wanted to focus, which is ironic, considering how important Eric would eventually become to me.

The day before my first Olympic race, I spent part of the morning listening to the U.S. grunge-rock band Soundgarden while riding the rollers. I trained again that afternoon on those cylinders, which allow you to pedal your bike while staying in the same place.

July 21 I was called to my race. I stood at the start line with fifty-seven other competitors, holding my bike. I felt calm, physically good but not great, and ready for the race to unfold, tactically focused on waiting for the right moment instead of using too much energy too soon. Then it started to rain—a thunderstorm—which I hate.

Less than 2 kilometres into the race, my teammate Linda Jackson crashed into a mailbox, badly injuring her arm. Now it was just Sue Palmer and me left for Team Canada.

At around 30 kilometres, three riders—one from Australia, one from France, one from Italy—staged a breakaway, creating a little gap in front of the peloton. Though it was early, I knew that if I didn't get up there in the next five minutes, I likely never would. An American and some others were also trying to make it into the breakaway group. At the feed zone, where support staff provided energy drinks and food, I heard athletes breathing hard and thought: *Now or never.* I attacked, making it into the lead group. With 60 kilometres remaining, the Australian rider dropped back, and I remember thinking: *Time to go.*

Jeannie Longo of France had been in front of the breakaway the whole time. Whenever I tried to pull through to take my turn in the lead, she attacked, so I decided to sit behind her, with the Italian rider sitting behind me. Longo was on fire. Drafting behind her felt like riding behind a 105-pound human motorcycle.

For most of the race, we had only a small margin on the peloton—I'm glad I didn't know how small. Since we weren't working as a team, those in the peloton could still catch us, and it wasn't until the last half-lap of the race that most of them gave up, allowing our lead to grow.

Longo attacked on the last hill. By then, I knew I wasn't going to win the Olympics, but I was determined not to lose a medal. I raced as hard as I could with the Italian rider—Imelda Chiappa—sitting behind, refusing to pull through. She passed me in the last 200 metres, taking the silver behind France. I crossed the finish knowing I'd won bronze.

I was euphoric, despite being soaking wet and exhausted. Wonder. Awe. Shock. *An Olympic medal!*

Mine was Canada's first medal at the Atlanta Olympics, and our first ever in women's cycling. It was a big deal. The media went wild, like nothing I'd experienced before. Instead of going back to warm down and recover, as I did after every race, I had to go here and there, talking about myself, something I'd never done before at that level. Though I'd always been good at expressing myself, I hadn't expected to be suddenly famous, and I knew none of this would help when I was back on my bike in my next race.

For an interview with CBC-TV's Brian Williams, the network had arranged for my parents to be connected with us live, via satellite, from the CBC station in Winnipeg. I sat in the Atlanta studio, hoping my dad would be sober, and that he wouldn't antagonize my mom. On the surface, we managed to look like a normal family, and since Brian later said he loved the interview, I didn't tell him how much I had agonized over those few minutes of airtime.

Because we cyclists couldn't train on the streets of Atlanta, our national team relocated to a university campus in Alabama. Everyone was thrilled for me, including racing legend Steve Bauer, winner of Canada's first Olympic medal in road cycling. I began by feeling great, but then I put my medal in the bottom of my suitcase and didn't look at it again until the Games were over. I didn't want to talk about what I had done, I wanted to focus on what I still had to do.

I had eleven days before my next race—the individual road time trial, a new Olympic event. Because of my bronze medal, I had graduated in many people's minds from "a possibility" to "a sure thing" for gold, creating an unbearably heavy burden of expectation. I remember thinking: *You have no right to tell me this. You have no idea how hard this is going to be. You have no idea how much I'm going to have to hurt myself.*

Mirek was in Atlanta though he had no status, and while he was not allowed into the Athletes' Village, he was allowed into the Alabama camp. For once, his negativity proved useful in countering all the overly optimistic predictions showered on me.

Each day I rode the rollers, had breakfast, trained on the road, then napped, then went back to the rollers again, which was essentially Mirek's program.

I was still convinced that eating very little was the key to success because it made me feel in control. I allowed myself one small bag of jelly beans as a treat each afternoon. I would watch the Olympics on TV while sorting the candies according to flavour. I would eat all of the same flavour in a single mouthful. This ritual, involving around thirty jelly beans, lasted about two hours.

I returned from the Alabama camp to the Athletes' Village two days before the time trial. It covered the same course as the road race, to be ridden twice. The day was so hot and humid that I think most of us were having an ugly ride. At one point, I remember thinking my head would explode in my helmet, forcing me to back off a little.

Each time I climbed the course hill, a young guy would run up beside me, faster than I was riding, shouting encouragement and thrusting a massive Canadian flag into the air. He made me push harder than I should have. It was all for me, and all for Canada. He was awesome!

During the first part of the second lap, I was afraid I would blow up, but then I recovered sufficiently to finish. I remember dismounting, slumping on the side of the road, face burning, perspiring profusely, thinking that I hadn't done enough. It took me a while to realize I had finished third.

Incredibly I'd won another bronze.

During the Closing Ceremony, I embraced the full spirit of the Olympics. Marathoner Josia Thugwane had become the first black South African to win gold in the first post-apartheid Games in which South Africa was allowed to compete. He accepted his medal in the midst of a cheering stadium. It was such an amazing moment.

I took the subway to downtown Atlanta, where I saw a big Nike ad announcing, "Silver Sucks!"

I thought, *Well, I must be a loser with only two bronze medals*.

That ad reminded me what I'd forgotten for a day: The Olympics are also a big circus.

Canada won five cycling medals in Atlanta, which beat our sport's all-time Olympic tally of four. On our return home, we were swept up in celebrations. Yet all it took was for one person to ask, "What do you *really* do when you're not training?" to reduce my achievements into hunks of bronze. I began to ask myself: *Who are you, and what do you really do?*

So, here I was, an Olympic medal winner, back at ground zero. My medals deepened my depression, because now I knew I was the same worthless person after Atlanta as I had been before.

I should have stopped my racing season right then, but instead I started training with Mirek for the World Championships in Switzerland.

Exhausted and full of despair, I began drinking again and doing drugs. Smoking, too. I was often wasted, wandering around in a zombie fog, partying too much, and staying up far too late. Instead of seeing myself as a triumphant Olympian, I had reverted to being that kid in the stairwell, guzzling whatever I could lay my hands on, consumed by misery, afraid to go home. My past still held me in its jaws, and cycling—with its stress, its commitment to pain, its crashes, and its crazy demand that I starve—was no solution.

I partied all night before a stage race in Vermont, returning to my condo an hour before start time. The next evening I was back at the bar, where a bunch of us got high on the recreational drug Ecstasy. When a teammate saw me, he joked, "What are you on, and where can I get some?"

I was smiling so much my eyes hurt. I drank three bottles of wine and smoked two packs of cigarettes and then some pot. In the morning, I missed my flight, so another cyclist drove me all the way back home to Hamilton. After flying high on Ecstasy for thirteen hours, I slept for two days.

When I arrived in Switzerland for the World Championships, Mirek complained that I wasn't focused, and he was right, but he did all of the wrong things to motivate me. When I failed to finish the road race, I told my mechanic that my bike didn't feel right. He replied, "That's because Mirek lowered your saddle."

When I confronted Mirek, he said, "I just wanted to see if you were too stupid to notice."

I was livid. I had paid to have Mirek travel with me, and I couldn't believe that he'd do something so foolishly underhanded. Discouraged, I called Eric Van den Eynde, our national team coach, confused about what I should do.

After Eric and I became friends, he would tell me, "You said, 'I don't know why, but I don't ride well anymore.' I asked if you were sick. You said no. I asked if you were tired. You said no. I came to realize that you had zero confidence. Here you were, this elite athlete, who was too afraid, too hurt, too damaged, too depressed to compete. When I suggested we work on ways to improve your leg speed, you replied, 'No, Mirek told me not to do that. I don't have much leg speed to begin with.' It was as if you'd been brainwashed, or put under a strange spell that made you miserable."

During all this time, the image of my sister, lying in despair on my father's couch, haunted me. At times, she seemed close enough to touch. I saw my father, steeped in alcohol, raging at the world for some unknown, unknowable offence. The darkness that lay in a sticky pool at my feet was creeping up my legs toward my vital organs, making me want to drink more, party harder. I didn't dare ask for help for fear that acknowledging these feelings might make me more vulnerable and let in more of the darkness.

I told myself: *You have to be stronger. You have to be better.* But I didn't know how.

My cycling career would grow even bleaker, but I was also about to find my miracle.

9

THE BREAKING POINT

I remember musing one day with my cycling friend Dede Demet about our idea of the perfect mate.

Dede said, "I'd like a very modern guy, someone who's well groomed and urbane."

I said, "I'd like a guy who's really fit and healthy, and who loves to be in the mountains."

Dede ended up with Michael Barry, who was exactly as she described. I ended up with Peter Guzmán, who was exactly as I described.

Peter and I met in September after the 1996 cycling season, when I was at an emotional low point.

I was visiting friends on a ranch in Oregon. Peter, as I would learn, had spent the summer in solitude at a base camp in the Lake Clark National Park and Preserve in Alaska. He'd arranged for a bush plane to drop him off with supplies at the confluence of Twin Lakes. He camped in a tent with a dilapidated cabin nearby to store his food supply as there were grizzly bears all around the area. An eighty-year-old man, a four-hour hike away, was his nearest neighbour. Now he was planning on visiting the same ranch and the same friends. When he heard a Canadian Olympic cyclist was visiting, he delayed his trip. He'd known too many athletes who wanted to talk only about their sport.

After Peter grew tired of waiting for me to leave, he chanced driving to the ranch. I remember seeing him in the doorway, carrying a bag of groceries, with a rolled bandana tied around his medium-length black hair. Since his parents were Mexican, he had a beautiful Latino look. *My god, he was cute!* I especially remember his arms—the most beautiful arms I've ever seen, with veins like a road map.

During our five days together, Peter and I went on long hikes and talked a lot, making a strong connection. As he told me, he had begun backpacking when he was sixteen: "On my first hike with a friend, it started to rain, hard. I was sitting by a stream in the deep forest, in my soaking clothes, thinking this was the most perfect experience ever. From that moment on, I always wanted to be out of the city, moving across the land, from place to place to place."

Soon Peter was hiking 385 miles over three or four weeks, driven by curiosity. "I was alone, just enjoying the miles, devouring them as I moved."

When he was twenty, he cycled across the United States, inspired by the book *Blue Highways* by William Least Heat-Moon. During a low point in that thirty-eight-year-old author's life, he had driven a van 13,000 miles along the rural American roads coloured blue in his Rand McNally atlas. Like Heat-Moon, Peter met many unusual people on his cycling journey, mostly from the hippie subculture. "Everybody made me feel good about America, while showing me different ways to live—healthy, free ways." This was important to Peter, since he'd heard only criticism of the United States as a kid travelling with his parents through Europe, causing him to wonder why the rest of the world hated Americans.

Peter's family also travelled to Mexico every year. These trips exposed him to poverty, which both scared and intrigued him. When he was older, he toured through Latin America, learning how generous and open people without wealth to protect could be.

I knew Peter was my kind of guy, and I felt sad when I had to leave to train for the 1997 summer season, not sure how, or if, we would reconnect. Though I really liked him, he was eleven years older—thirty-five to my twenty-four—and I imagined he thought I was too young and silly and underdeveloped.

Our mutual friend, attempting to matchmake, asked what I thought of Peter. I laughed. "You're joking, right?"

I was surprised when, shortly after our parting, I received a letter from him.

Clara, I really enjoyed your company, and I'm sad we're not going to be able to do together all those things we talked about, like baking bread and making pesto.

I thought: *Wow, he kind of likes me.* I wrote back, and we corresponded casually. He wrote:

Clara, Thanks for writing back. It's sort of an odd day here in Halfway, Oregon. Rain showers turned the foot and a half of snow in the valley into a thick bowl of mashed potatoes big enough to feed the world. Everyone's invited, but they're asked to bring their own sour cream and chives. Coming?

In December 1996, after I had returned to Hamilton, I received a letter from Peter telling me that he was planning a walk in Mexico's Baja California peninsula early in the new year. *A walk? What the hell is that?* I was mentally in a bad place, depressed about my weight and life in general, and Peter's letter brought me back to the peace and beauty of the ranch in Oregon. I thought: *Maybe this is supposed to be special.*

I was spending Christmas that year with my old roommate and friend Catrien Bouwman in Meaford, near Georgian Bay in Ontario. I read Peter's letter to Catrien, then asked, "What do you think about this guy?"

She said, "Clara, you have to find out who this person is. Just go."

So, I left for Boise, Idaho, which was the closest town to Halfway, Oregon, where Peter was spending the winter. We had about a week before he left for Baja. We talked and walked and talked some more, and he introduced me to car camping in his 1973 Volkswagen bus. When we drove into the forest, I was agog. "We're going to sleep here? What if an animal comes?"

Peter looked at me as if to say, *Are you for real?* but patiently reassured me we'd be fine.

And, of course, we were. I really liked camping, and he appreciated that I was so open to everything.

Peter was born in Albany, Oregon, in 1961, the youngest of three children. Though his father, Elías, was also American-born, he had grown up on a ranch in the Mexican state of Michoacán. When Elías was only eight, some men arrived to steal his father's horse. Elías heard shots fired and found his father dead on the porch. He had only a grade-two education. With his father gone, the ranch family was more vulnerable: cows, pigs, and other animals were being stolen on a regular basis. His mother had no choice but to leave. She took her children to Mexico City.

Peter's mother, Graciela Micaela Bravo De La Campa, also known as Mica, grew up in Mexico City, the daughter of an esteemed family that owned and operated two large movie theatres in the capital. Mica had a university degree. Her sister had one of the first motorcycle licenses issued to a female.

Elías met Mica while working in a billiard hall, one of the family's other businesses. They fell in love and were married. Elías couldn't legally work in Mexico because of his American citizenship, so they moved to Oregon and started their family. Elías found a job in a plywood mill, where he worked most of his life. He loved hard labour and refused to retire until he was sixty-five.

Peter was raised speaking Spanish to his mother and English to his father. He received a degree in telecommunications at Oregon State University. For the next decade, he worked three and a half to four months a year during the winter seasons at ski resorts. The rest of the year was free to travel. He chose this lifestyle and though it was difficult stretching the money for that many months, he didn't see it as hardship. On the contrary, he lived a very creative, unique, and deeply rewarding life on the road.

Peter worked enough to travel and didn't see the need to work more only to follow a lifestyle dictated by society. He never had a problem getting a job after months of bike touring in places like Pakistan, South and Central America, Europe, and North Africa, or distance hiking the Pacific Crest and Continental Divide Trails. While working, he skied over a hundred days a winter. I'd never met anyone like him.

During our week together in Halfway, Peter and I talked about all aspects of our lives and shared simple things, like cooking together. He was the most beautiful human being I'd ever met. His experiences, from an early age, had helped him develop great compassion for those struggling to live decent lives.

I enjoyed being with Peter, even though his good energy couldn't change my sense that I was unworthy. I still felt shitty inside.

Because I didn't know how to express my feelings, on our second-to-last day together, I wrote Peter a letter telling him how I felt about him.

He replied, "Clara, I feel the same about you."

Peter left, his backpack loaded for his Baja walk, and I returned to training, with the idea of trying to be an athlete again—not because I wanted that but because I was still under contract to the Saturn Cycling Team. To vicariously share Peter's journey, I bought the book *Into a Desert Place: A 3000 Mile Walk around the Coast of Baja California* by Graham Mackintosh. Since Mackintosh was a novice, he invariably got into difficulties. I would worry about Peter until I received yet another fantastic six- or seven-page handwritten letter, telling stories about the people he'd met, their culture, and the landscape, using every centimetre of every page. Each of Peter's letters gave me such a lift. They took me away from the racing that I had come to hate, letting me spend time with someone I was happy to know, who was doing something so exciting, something so private, while I was always exposed to public scrutiny.

That spring, one of Peter's special letters arrived in Hamilton after I had moved to California to train with my Saturn teammates. A friend couriered it to me in California but it went to the wrong address. I was about to leave to race with Saturn in New Zealand, and I wanted that letter. I *needed* that letter, and I needed it *immediately*. I went to the address where I was told it had been delivered and saw it lying on the doorstep—*my* letter—so I took it and read it. That moment—reading Peter's beautiful letter—was one of the few completely happy moments I would have for quite a long time.

During the Women's Tour of New Zealand, held outside of Hamilton, New Zealand, I was abruptly reminded—as so often before—of the cruelty of cycling.

My teammate Dede (Demet) Barry and I, along with Ina Teutenberg, who was on the German national team, were working together to catch the peloton. As we took a corner on a steep descent, travelling about 60 kilometres an hour, we suddenly saw the mangled bodies of a dozen riders strewn along the road and against the guardrail.

Dede made it around the crash, but because people were crossing the road to help the injured, Ina and I had nowhere to go. When I tried to weave through the crowd, I T-boned a South African rider, jettisoning off my bike like Superman flying through the air.

I scrambled upright thinking, *Maybe I'm okay*. Then I noticed blood. I took off my Oakley sunglasses. They were filled with more blood. I threw my glasses to the ground and started screaming, because I'd always dreaded cutting my face.

Ina, who'd had military training as a nurse, saw I was going into shock. Though she's smaller than I am, she grabbed me by the arms and told me: "Clara, you're hurt, but you're going to be fine."

She picked up my glasses and my bike. Though my front brake had shifted, it was okay.

Ina said, "Now, go. Ride. Finish."

I travelled the rest of the 10 kilometres on that bike, head throbbing, face gashed, blood flowing. Our team director, René Wenzel, who is a large, strong man, turned pale at the sight of me. That's when I started bawling, the wound still gaping.

At the nearest small-town clinic, the doctor told us, "I have to be honest. I usually work on animals. I think you should go to the city."

I was driven to Hamilton, New Zealand, in an ambulance. Another girl was lying beside me—an Aussie with a broken collarbone. She was moaning. "I used to be so strong. Now I might not be able to race."

I stared at her with my hemorrhaging face. "Are you fucking crazy?" I asked her. "Be grateful you're alive!"

She couldn't seem to understand that life meant more than any stupid bike race.

The surgeon stitched up my face so deftly that I escaped with only the smallest of scars. At an eleven-hour stopover in the Los Angeles airport on my flight home, some guy who'd been staring at my black eye and stitched and swollen face asked, "What bastard did that to you?"

That "bastard" was bike racing.

Back in Hamilton, Ontario, I learned that Peter was in Tijuana, having completed his incredible solo adventure. I convinced him to fly to Toronto, then picked him up at the airport in a truck borrowed from my old roommate Tracy Jolley. Peter was exhausted from his walk through the sparse desert, while I was struggling to train and to race while deeply depressed. My face had healed, but my spirit was broken. We took it easy, strolling around town, buying fresh fruits and vegetables, cooking delicious meals, still trying to figure out who each other was, and how we might fit together. The last thing I wanted was to train. All I could think about was being with Peter, the one and only positive element in my life.

One day Peter and I drove to Peterborough in Tracy's rusted-out truck for a criterium in nearby Bobcaygeon. I remember sitting in the cab, parked in front of the house where we were staying, waiting for the keys to arrive and drinking wine from a disposable water bottle that Peter had cut in half. I came third in the criterium, racing against the men, winning eighty dollars, which I used to buy a Peugeot pepper grinder. I still have it.

Since I wanted Peter to meet Mirek, I invited my coach for dinner. Mirek refused even to acknowledge Peter's presence. Instead, he talked over him without looking at him or asking him any questions. This was a side of Mirek I hadn't seen before—or, if I had, I'd refused to register it. It was so weird, watching the evening unfold.

Afterward, Peter asked, "Who is that guy? He has such bad energy." He didn't say anything more. He didn't have to, because his remarks suddenly jarred me into seeing Mirek through Peter's objective eyes, along with those of so many others around me.

After Peter left, though, I continued to train with Mirek, who seemed to want complete control over me. I felt ridiculed, fat, and worthless, because of both his words and the way he looked at me. I had heard from other cyclists about using bulimia to control weight, so I tried to make myself throw up, but I couldn't even do that. I was a failed bulimic.

Because of chronic ankle pain, I commuted two hours each way to a physiotherapist in Mississauga. I'm guessing now that nothing was wrong with my ankle. My head, my heart, and my spirit were wounded, but instead of admitting that, I found it easier to manifest physical pain.

Unlike Peter's romantic experiences in off-road America, the ones I endured while training with Mirek were neither inspiring nor even palatable. My mind was often on Peter, who continued to write letter after letter, inviting me to Oregon. Meanwhile, I filled page after page in my journal with dark stories of my numbing journey to nowhere.

April 18, 1997

Another cheap motel room, another small-town USA. The glamorous life of a bike racer. Yeah, right. . . . I wonder how individuals who spend so much time alone will exist with one another. Finding the balance between the solitude, which is necessary in doses, and the potentially wonderful togetherness will be a necessary search.

April 19, 1997

Sitting here in this room again. All I want is to go home, be home. The fatigue of yesterday, the pain of today. I am expecting some spark of motivation when the racing begins. Cannot wait to sleep.

May 14, 1997

Going through the motions of missing someone is difficult. I spoke to Peter twice already, and the sweet sound of his voice and calming demeanour remind me of how fortunate I am to know this beautiful man. Thoughts of how much longer I will do this—how much longer I will race—have been prevalent throughout this tour. My soul is elsewhere. The hotel is musty and damp. The sounds of the streets float up through the window.

I decided to slip away, without Mirek's knowledge, to visit Peter in Halfway, Oregon.

May 20, 1997; Baker City, Oregon

Feeling lucky to be here—rest, relaxation and recovery. My only stress is the call I must make to good old Mirek. He'll be pissed that I am here, and no matter what explanation I give, he won't understand this journey, this escape into a world that is so necessary, while I'm subjected to the chaos of competition and the superficial world of sport, a small and false world. Waiting to see Peter's smile, to feel his positive energy.

May 24, 1997; Halfway, Oregon

Peter walks in the room—my flying body hitting him at the door! Music, red wine, and the sound of rain on the window. What I will do for the remainder of this wonderful (potentially) stay is to savour every moment.

Back in training, my dark thoughts suffocated any sense of peace or achievement.

June 3, 1997

Why do I despise my body so? Why do I feel trapped under these layers of flesh? I cannot accept this physical being as it is. I am disgusted by my lack of self-control, disgusted at the rolls of flesh that cover my body. It hurts me, and I feel guilt for my lack of self-worth, hinging on my body-fat count. LET THESE FEELINGS GO so I can feel the freedom of being. I want to live. Perhaps it is time to begin to try. . . . I feel fortunate to be loved. To be loved by my family, my friends. To feel the intimacy with Peter, and to begin to share my deep-down feelings with another.

June 8, 1997

Back in the slums of Kutztown, Pennsylvania. I continue to question my longevity within this athletic go-around. How much longer will I stay within this mundane mindset? Day by day. Hour by hour. Minute by minute.

One day, when Mirek and I were driving through Kutztown to our training camp, we passed a street person with long hair.

Mirek turned from the front seat to exclaim, "Hey, Clara, there's your boyfriend!"

I stared at him: *There's no way you could have said that.* I asked him to repeat himself.

He said, "That homeless guy—he looks like the guy you're seeing."

That jibe cut me to the core. I thought: *No fucking more!*

•　　•　　•

In our Pennsylvania training camp, Mirek continued to harp on my weight. My teammate Dede remembers my taking some cheese out of the refrigerator and Mirek shouting from across the room, "Look at that fat ass taking out her fucking cheese from the fucking fridge!"

Dede was shocked, even though she added, "Mirek was kind of laughing when he said it." She also confirmed that Mirek had been unhappy when she started dating Michael Barry, her husband-to-be, because he believed her attention would no longer be entirely focused on training.

It was obvious that Mirek cared only about winning, which was not a good enough reason for me to be racing. Someone who is successful is supposed to be happy, but cycling—the training, the culture, and the lifestyle—fed my negativity and despair. I made up my mind to cut ties with Mirek and to leave the sport that had defined my life for eight years. I just didn't know how or when to go about it.

July 19, 1997

Back home to Hamilton with Mirek. Don't want to deal with him, but know I must. I want to be left alone, to face things head on, not hide from them. I'll try my best. I must be solid. Strong. I must be ME!

July 21, 1997

Spoke to Mirek this morning. He said his usual, about how I should not leave the training because it will be difficult to come back into it. Wanted me to come to his altitude camp in September. I said no. I stood up for myself and spoke my thoughts. He shot some of them down, but I didn't cave. I know realistically we will not work together in the future. He works hard and gives a lot, but I will not deal with his games anymore, or his ego, or his jealousy when I take someone else's advice. I do not have the energy, and it is my responsibility to get out of this constantly intense competitive atmosphere which is sucking the life out of me.

I was ready to move on, while still acknowledging the great debt I owed to Mirek. He had been there from the beginning. He had chal-

lenged me, made me want to be good at something. That was important to me, because everything had always been so shitty. It's hard to
believe anyone else would have been as intense or as committed to me
as Mirek. He wanted me to be good for him, and only for him, but that
was my problem to work through, not his. Mirek forced me to change,
and I'm grateful for that. Maybe the training didn't have to be as brutal
as it was, but considering how aimless and lost I was, maybe it did. I
understand how some might see this as a rationalization, but though
I struggled while training with Mirek, I also struggled with everything
before Mirek. Everything I continued to deal with as a person was in
place before Mirek, and I was the one who played it out through him.

I flew to Winnipeg to spend two days with my family. While I was glad
to be going home, I knew from past experience that two days would be
a half-day too long. It was wearying listening to old complaints, with me
as a reasonably fresh audience. On these visits, my dad often insisted on
taking me to his pub to show me off to his friends. Though they were
decent, hard-working people, I resented them, and the pub environment, for feeding him the booze that kept his alcoholism alive. To this
day, bars make me cringe.

On this trip, as on all others, I smiled and smiled throughout my
duty visits, wishing everyone would shut up.

I had one official task: the July 22 opening of the Clara Hughes
Children's Playground. I was swamped with kids who wanted to see
my medals. When I said, "Touch them, feel them," they were surprised.
Innocent faces. Innocent eyes. Some gave me gifts of plastic jewellery. I
felt strange, almost embarrassed to have this park named for me, though
I was glad the kids would have a place to play. I'd prepared a speech but
scrapped it, letting the words flow from my heart. I even saw a few tears
in the audience.

After that came the unveiling of the plaque, with me carved in
bronze. Strange indeed!

•　•　•

To my surprise, the person I most wanted to consult about my relationship with Mirek was my dad. He had always given me good, useful advice. He understood that the bridge between Mirek and me was broken, and that trying to rebuild it would be fruitless.

My dad's advice was this: "There's no reasoning with a person like that. You can't talk to him. Writing a letter is the best you can do."

I composed the letter, then read it to my dad. He helped me get the words—and the emotions within the words—just right. I dropped the letter into the post and waited.

After a few days, the phone rang.

It was Mirek. He called me a coward, then said, "Burn in hell!"

It was terrible, but it was over.

10

APPLYING THE BRAKES

I was due to train with our national team in a camp in Victoria. While in the bathroom of the Vancouver airport, waiting for my connecting flight, I felt an enormous weight descend upon me. I went into one of the stalls and cried uncontrollably, with waves of misery passing over me. I didn't know where I was. I didn't know who I was. I felt fat and out of shape, and I couldn't face having to train where people would see me. I was also suffering chronic pain in my ankle, now diagnosed as tendinitis.

At the camp, I went for my scheduled physical with Gloria Cohen, the team doctor. Sensing my inner distress, she asked, "Clara, what's going on? You seem sad. Do you want to talk about it?"

I started to cry again. I told her I didn't know what was wrong, but that I couldn't train.

She replied, "There are ways to deal with this." She talked about depression, medication, and other options.

I told myself: *I'm not like that. I'm not one of those people.* I insisted aloud, "I'm not depressed."

I left Dr. Cohen on a wave of righteous indignation: *Who gave her permission to decide something is wrong with me?*

But there *was* something wrong. I knew I couldn't train the way I was used to training—all-out, all the time—and I could no longer blame Mirek for the emptiness and self-hatred I carried inside. The one positive in my life remained Peter.

I returned to Hamilton, midsummer 1997, loaded up Tracy's pickup truck with my cycling clothes, my winner's jerseys, my team uniforms, and my other cycling stuff, which I never wanted to see again, and I donated them to charity. I told my Saturn team that I needed a sick leave because of chronic tendinitis, then joined Peter in California to start a new life.

Peter had introduced me to the high-altitude desert town of Bishop, California, within sight of the Sierra Nevada and White Mountains. We rented a cabin, then furnished it with old junky belongings, purchased at the yard sale of a local mountaineer. He'd died in a climbing accident. which, tragically, was not uncommon in that area. For a bed, we used our thin Therm-a-Rest backpacking sleeping pads.

Looking back, I realize the sacrifice he made. Instead of living his passion for travel, he stayed with me, doing everything from laundry at a local laundromat to grocery shopping to riding thousands of training miles at my side. He allowed me to prepare for the upcoming season, and tried to pull me out of the dark draw of emotions I couldn't hide very well.

Everything quieted down for me after the relentless, mad swirl of competitive racing. I shared with Peter the Canadian authors with whom I'd grown up—Michael Ondaatje, Al Purdy, and Margaret Laurence, especially her travel book *The Prophet's Camel Bell: A Memoir of Somaliland*, which I believe to be one of the best ever written. Peter introduced me to Jack Kerouac, Hunter S. Thompson, and the philosophies of Bruce Lee. Most important, he shared the writings of Joseph Campbell, who has had a huge impact on me to this day.

Once I was away from the toxic environment of cycling, my tendon rapidly healed, indicating this was a psychological injury that had manifested physically. Peter and I did a ten-day trek on the John Muir Trail in the High Sierras, just the two of us, dipping our toes into that sea of high-altitude granite. It was my first distance hike, covering about 265 kilometres—through magnificent snow-capped peaks, reflective lakes, cascading rivers, and fragrant pine groves, all above 8000 feet, ending on Mount Whitney up at 14500 feet.

Peter and I grew close, very close. We shared the same values. We both disliked structure and routine. We both were physical, with a zestful curiosity about life. While I was socially outgoing, Peter was quieter, which made us a balanced team. I would like to say I was blissfully happy. That I had peace of mind. But, though I loved Peter, I couldn't escape myself. On the deepest level, everything was just a distraction from the sadness and loneliness that still weighed me down. At times, I felt like I was sitting on a time bomb.

After I told my dad about Peter, he was excited to meet this person with whom his daughter was enamoured, so he visited us for a week in Bishop. It wasn't long before he was rearranging our cabin and making a huge mess of our kitchen. I remember waking one morning to find he'd been up for hours, nailing all our utensils to the wall, creating big holes. I told him, "Dad, Peter and I live here. It's a collective thing. You can't just rearrange the place when you feel like it."

After I took down all our utensils, Dad was angry, but he got over it, and when I drove him to the Reno airport, he gave me an unexpected gift. He told me, "Clara, whatever you do, don't try to change Peter. He's a prince, the best of the best."

Considering how most fathers would view our alternative lifestyle, that's pretty remarkable. It was also an honest reflection of my dad's values. I appreciated that he understood Peter, and ever afterward, whenever we spoke he asked, "How is that prince doing?"

By now, I'd also had a chance to meet Peter's parents, Elías and Mica. While I was cycling in Oregon, they had come to watch me race, and later I visited them in Albany with Peter. I loved them immediately, and they were proud of my achievements. Peter's father took me to the barbershop, to the grocery store, to the bank, wanting me to show people my Olympic medals and saying, "This is Clara, she's my Peter's girlfriend."

Peter's parents were Mexican Catholic, so Elías made sure I knew I would be sleeping on the fold-out bed in the living room, while Peter would be sleeping in his own bedroom—no unmarried cohabiting in his house!

Peter's brother, Michael, was a lawyer, and his sister, Vivian, was raising a family in Italy. By the time Peter, the youngest, had come along, I believe his parents were somewhat tired of parenting, so they didn't have many photos of him growing up, though I saw a lot of his siblings. This worked out well enough for Peter, since he had more freedom to do what he wanted, just as I had. Luckily for his parents, he made healthy choices. Mica could see that Peter was happy, and she always encouraged him by saying in Spanish: *"Quinto que tengo, quinto que gasto,"* which translates to, "A nickel I have, a nickel I spend." Through her family's business, she had experienced too many times people who were only too willing to find ways to get at your savings. She said it was better to spend and enjoy what you have. Why save all that money, then worry about investments that usually turn into losses?

Elías had had trouble accepting Peter's lifestyle, but I believe he appreciated him more because he could see how much Peter's support contributed to my success. Elías loved sports and he was so proud of everything we achieved. Though Peter and I weren't dependent on our parents' approval, it felt good to have it.

I returned to cycling for the 1998 season and managed two months of racing before I had to quit again. The prior season's accident in New Zealand had made me realize once more the physical and emotional toll cycling could take. I also remembered the conversation I'd had with our national team doctor, when she'd asked if I was suffering from depression. Though I had vehemently denied all possibility of that, I began to acknowledge that this word might describe the sadness and loneliness and despair that sometimes overwhelmed me, even when I should have been happiest. I felt a strong need to step away from sport in order to heal myself, both mentally and physically.

I bought a vintage trailer, a 1957 Corvette, for $350, then spent another $1000 for material and a carpenter to help me restore it. I was a dreamer, free from sport for the first time in my adult life. I thought Peter and I could live on the road in our silver bubble. It was 11 by 7 feet, perfect for our minimalistic lifestyle. We pulled it behind a Toyota pickup, which I bought second-hand, then parked it with friends in Bishop when we weren't camping in California's vast national forests and open spaces.

Back in Bishop, Peter and I talked about what we wanted to do— perhaps travel to Nepal or India. We bought an armload of books and read voraciously about places that might provide a fresh start. We painted a friend's house for money and saved our cash. It was then that Peter persuaded me to try something new—something I never thought I would, should, or could do: a bike tour strictly for pleasure.

We decided on a four-day trip into Death Valley. I laid out the gear I thought necessary, ready to pack it in panniers on the sides, rear, front, and handlebars of my bike, as required. Then I looked at the small pile of stuff Peter was planning to take. Typically, he would never impose instructions on me, since everyone was supposed to learn by example. This time, I insisted, "C'mon, I'm your girlfriend!" He helped me pare down to *one* set of camp clothes, *one* set of cycling clothes, and so on, till I needed only rear panniers.

We pulled out around noon.

From elite Tour de France competitor I had morphed into Tour de Dirt tourist—what a comedown! I still feared the worst, trying to squeeze fun out of a sport I'd come to loathe seemed impossible, but I was wrong. Those first few miles were special. My reluctance turned to relief, then to excitement. Who knew cycling could be fun? No training schedule. No push, no pressure. No Mirek yelling "Harder! Faster!" Just enjoying the adventure.

South of Bishop, a narrow road leads east in the barren high desert of the Inyo mountain range. Piñon trees and sagebrush dot the landscape, with the occasional juniper tree. After the long climb up smooth pavement, the pavement ends at the turnoff to distant Saline Valley. We descended 35 miles on a rough, single-lane track of rock and boulders, passing through huge ranges turned purple by the heavy evening sun.

I felt euphoric.

Our goal was the hot springs in Saline Valley—a small ramshackle settlement of school buses turned campers and canvas tents. Technically part of Death Valley National Park, back then it was cared for and maintained by a tiny fringe subculture of older hippies.

Arriving in Saline Valley was like stepping into another world, one teeming with people, some clothed, others comfortably nude. It was fun in its own way, but we were no longer alone.

Other bike trips followed, including desert camping through Baja California's peninsula. For six weeks we cycled through the remote dirt roads of the interior peninsula, then rough coastal roads. We camped under the stars every night. We cooked over small fires for all our meals. It was these six weeks of peaceful, magical, remote travel that gave me the clarity and resolve to pursue cycling again.

I thought of all the stupid things I'd done while training, and how the whole process had been so intrinsically wrong. I realized that an athlete could train in many different ways. I realized cycling could be fun and fulfilling, and training for it could be done in a positive way, not the way I'd known before. I wanted to race again.

In a quiet moment, I said to Peter, "I think I can do this, and I think I can do it right."

Though he was disappointed that I would be leaving him and the trip, he understood that my mind was made up, so he encouraged me, as always. While he continued his tour, I returned to Bishop, where I would live all winter in the Corvette trailer, parked behind a friend's garage. It became my base for training as a cyclist again.

My comeback ride was with the Saturn team at California's Redlands Classic, an elite four-day stage race covering approximately 350 miles with the field limited to two hundred entrants. Though I did well in that race, afterward I exhausted myself by overtraining, pushing myself too hard, too long, too much. So much for coaching myself—I was as bad as Mirek! Instead, I started working with Eric Van den Eynde. After I'd won my second medal in Atlanta, Eric had taken me aside to say, "You know, you could be even better than you are."

I had thought: *Fuck you, pal, I won two bronze medals!*

Looking back, I now understood Eric was trying to tell me that Mirek's training was exhausting me and making me too dependent.

As he later explained: "You were like a person in a cast. Someone incapable of thinking freely. Mirek gave you great endurance, and that will never leave you. Now you can do anything you want, but you have to learn—*we* have to learn—*why* you are good, *how* you are good, and what it will take to get you to believe in yourself."

Eric treated every rider as an individual. He had a brother, two years older, who had loved to race until his coach drove him into the ground by mocking him—"I thought you were tough, but I guess I was wrong." Eric's brother lost all of his confidence, and then took years to recover emotionally.

Eric was determined not to do that to any rider. I had a day off every week and worked with specific intensity rather than volume. Training with Eric was a gift. As he liked to say, "To improve, you have to do one thing you like, and two you don't like, every day."

That made sense. Since I lacked confidence as a sprinter, I had avoided it. Now I didn't.

Eric was my anti-Mirek. He used a philosopher's touch to communicate, and he was genuine when he said, "Clara, I don't care if you choose not to race. I only care that you're okay." Eric had a huge impact on me as an athlete and a human being.

In spring 1999, I went to Europe for the cycling season—Belgium, France, Italy. Peter and I kept in touch by phone, letters, and e-mails. He was amazed he'd found a partner more transient than he was.

Peter described his adventures, the homey details of life in Bishop, quoted wise words of support, and told me how much he missed his "green-eyed, Canadian woman with the wild red hair." He also began to think about a trip of his own. With no other plan than to cycle down the Baja Peninsula in Mexico, it organically unfolded into a great five-month-long tour, ending in the Yukon's Dawson City. All unplanned and completely spontaneous.

April 16, 1999

Hello Clara,

8 a.m. 48F, calm, a light blanket of cirrus clouds. Another pretty morning in the Sierra foothills. Plenty of bird activity. Quail, a Blackbird carrying off straw, the House Finch couple busy flying in and out of the birdhouse in the front yard, a Flicker scooting up the light pole. White-crowned Sparrows

everywhere. The no-nonsense bobcat walks by the front yard on his morning
rounds to who knows where . . .

Bruce Lee wants to add a bit here: "Training deals not with an object, but
with the human spirit and human emotions."

Miss you much. Love, Peter

April 21, 1999

I painted all the rust spots on my mountain bike with an anti-rust paint. Can't
say it looks too neat but it'll preserve the frame for another tour along the coasts
of Baja . . .

I think of you constantly Clara, wondering how you are doing during the
day. Sleeping alone is no good without you . . .

April 23, 1999

Well, I miss you more than ever. We are always changing, both when together
and apart, and so does our relationship. And though I feel blue, I have much
satisfaction knowing you are enjoying yourself right now. . . . I look back on my
Alaskan experiences and recall many times when I'd literally burst out laughing
(joy is what Thoreau calls it) because the beauty surrounding me at the moment
was more than I could take.

April 28, 1999

Here's a quote I thought you'd like by H. G. Wells: "Every time I see an
adult on a bicycle, I no longer despair for the future of the human race."

April 30, 1999

So I cracked The Klondike Fever *by Pierre Berton, published in 1958.*
The language and the style is old like the book, and I must say it's wonderfully
done. The oldness is the flavor, not a distraction. . . . When you read it, you
will want to experience the Yukon even more. The Yukon, the Baja of Canada.

•   •   •

Though racing was as hard as ever, others began to notice that I was cycling with a smile, and in June 1999, I had something to smile about: I won gold in the national road race in Sherbrooke, Quebec—by ten minutes! Though I was working with Saturn, for me it felt like an 83-kilometre solo ride through soaring temperatures, thinking *focus-focus-focus,* pacing myself, making sure I didn't kill my legs by using too big a gear, making sure I had enough fuel. That translated into two bottles in the last five laps, an energy bar, and three gels (energy packets of concentrated carbohydrates).

I couldn't wait for the World Championships in 1999, to be held in Verona, Italy, where Peter would be joining me. I felt motivated. I felt in tune with my training. I found it difficult to believe that I had been willing to give up on this only a year ago.

World, here I come!

When I unpacked my time-trial bike on site, one of our Canadian coaches, Yury Kashirin, noticed my front brake wasn't set right. Apparently, the cable that applied pressure to the brake pad had popped out during the flight.

Since the rear brake worked fine, I told him, "Ah, don't worry, I'll be okay."

"Are you sure?"

I was so excited to get moving, brake cable or no, that I replied, "Yeah, it's fine."

Reluctantly, he let me go.

I've been hit by cars three times. In 1992, I was in Allentown, Pennsylvania, when a woman sped ahead of our team, then slammed on her brakes. Everyone swerved around the car but me. I launched into the air, landing with enough force to break my tailbone. I wanted to beat the living crap out of her, but fortunately the others held me back.

Three weeks later, I was racing in Hamilton when a woman ran a red light. After I saw her go for it, I started sprinting, but she nailed my back wheel and I flew into the air yet again.

She was very apologetic. I took her name. My bike was totalled, and she told me she'd pay for the repairs.

I followed through, collecting estimates.

My mom

My dad during his military days

My parents' wedding

My mom towing Dodie and me

Dodie holding me

Dad and me

Me at age four

Me and my friend Julie Slessor
posing with my bike

My tenth birthday

Me at age thirteen

Dodie, Dad,
and me

With my sister,
Dodie, during
better days

With National Team Directeur Sportif Denis Roux at the Tour Cycliste Féminin, 1994

A low point: post-crash and mid-depression, Women's Tour of New Zealand, 1997

With Nicole Reinhart (second from right) in the Sea Otter Classic in California, 2000

My second Olympic medal (bronze) at the Atlanta Olympics, 1996 (*The Canadian Press*)

Celebrating my second bronze medal of the 1996 Atlanta Olympics with my coach Mirek Mazur; his wife, Eva; and CBC Television's Ron Hayman (standing)

With Big Dodie

Peter at age sixteen, Oregon

My mother- and father-in-law, Mica and Elías Guzmán

Me and Peter on my first bike tour into Saline Valley, 1998

ABOVE: Wedding
ceremony (our
witnesses from
left to right, Steve
Anderson and Eric
Van den Eynde)

RIGHT: Our wedding
cake

Honeymoon on
the Dempster
Highway, 2002

Her husband phoned to say, "We won't be paying. My wife didn't run the light."

Since I was twenty, just trying to get by, I phoned the woman to tell her, "I hope you feel good about yourself. I'm a poor athlete, and now I have no bike."

When I won bronze at the Atlanta Olympics four years later, I thought about her even while I was on the podium: *Now do you know whose bike you totalled, you cheater and liar!*

But, back to Italy . . . I was going down the course, feeling great, when, suddenly, an Italian woman passed me in her little car. When she slammed on her brakes to turn left, I tried to stop, forgetting my brakes were faulty. I hit her car, then flew across the road, my arms fanning out like those of a cliff diver. I hit the curb, hard, then lay still.

The woman climbed out of her car, screaming, because she thought she'd killed me.

All I could think was: *You fucking bitch!*

At that moment, I was mainly pissed off about her interrupting my cycling when I'd felt so good, instead of appreciating that I was still alive. It was only later that I remembered the Australian cyclist in the ambulance in New Zealand, and my advice to her: *Be grateful, stupid!*

By now Yuri was also on the scene, shrieking. People were pouring out of cafés and shops, causing a huge commotion. Someone brought me water.

The next day I couldn't lift my arms, but I still raced in the time trial, finishing fifth. I tried the road race but had to quit partway through.

That was it for me at the Worlds in Italy, which was to have been my triumphant comeback. Peter had been there to cheer me on, along with his mother, Mica; his sister, Vivian; and her sons, Michael and Nicholas, who lived there.

I set my sights on the 2000 Sydney Olympics.

11

SYDNEY OLYMPICS 2000

In July 2000, I qualified for the Sydney Olympics to be held in the fall; unfortunately, this victory came with a disheartening sidebar.

At the 1999 World Championships, I was supposed to room with a young Quebec cyclist, Geneviève Jeanson. She chose instead to stay with her coach, André Aubut. Geneviève seemed like a nice kid, and in Italy she won both the Junior Women's road race and the Junior Women's time trial, while I was a podium no-show.

In the 2000 individual road time trial held in Peterborough, Ontario, Geneviève and I would be racing against each other. I was the defending national time-trial champion, and she was a rising star—the old guard versus the new, as some saw it, though to me it was just another race I was determined to win.

We would be cycling 26 kilometres over rolling hills and fast new pavement, without much wind. With only 1 kilometre to go, I was in the lead, and Geneviève was second. As I made my last left-hand turn, I saw a pickup truck in my lane. The road was supposed to be closed to traffic, but there it was. The marshals frantically directed me to the other side of the barricades. Swerving around the truck took me off course in the home stretch and toward oncoming traffic. In spite of that, I hit the finish line six seconds ahead of Geneviève. The race commissaires assured me: "We saw what happened. We have your time."

Afterward, Geneviève's coach protested the result. He claimed I'd used the draft from the cars to propel me to the finish line. Of course, that was absurd. I'd have had to have been mad to attempt to gain an advantage by putting myself in the line of traffic.

The officials consulted their rule books, even measured the final kilometre of the course, before rejecting Aubut's protest. In fact, they confirmed that I had covered a longer distance, into oncoming traffic, suffering a disadvantage rather than an advantage.

At the presentations, the third-place winner was called to the podium, then Geneviève in second place. Her dad held her back, still refusing to accept the results. I said to her, "C'mon, Geneviève. You're not really going to do this, are you?"

She glanced at me, then at her dad, in complete confusion. Finally, she stepped onto the podium, while her coach continued to rant to the press.

This had been my best time trial since my bronze-medal race in Atlanta. Because Geneviève later won the road race, we both qualified for the Sydney Olympics, along with Lyne Bessette, who was selected as the third rider.

Of course, none of this was on my mind in the summer of 2000 as I prepared for the Olympics. In August, a month before the Games, I had ridden the women's Tour de France (renamed the Grande Boucle Féminine Internationale, meaning the "great loop"). It was hot, hilly, and rainy, and I was deathly ill. I remember being in Lourdes with Dede Barry and coughing uncontrollably, which was ironic, given Lourdes's reputation as a place of miraculous healing. I couldn't breathe. I couldn't sleep. I quit the Tour on the seventh day, then travelled to the national team condo in Bromont, Quebec, to recover from what turned out to be whooping cough. One time I woke up gagging, and Peter was ready to call the ambulance, not knowing if I could breathe. He didn't know that the gagging would happen whenever I did any intense training. He also didn't know how to call an ambulance in Canada!

When I told Eric how bad it was, he said, "Given what you've come through, no one deserves to go to the Olympics more than you. You never know what's going to happen on any day. You're so good at this sport that your chances of having *that* day, in which everything comes together, are better than for most."

I flew to Sydney. Doctors gave me puffers, but I still felt awful as I boarded the plane, coughing and hacking, and wondering what the hell I was doing.

The Games ran from September 15 to October 1—the XXVII Olympiad, with teams from 199 countries, the most ever, but with Afghanistan banned due to the Taliban's oppression of women.

The Opening Ceremony began by recognizing Australia's pastoral heritage and the importance of the seas to her coastal dwellers. Then came the influx of immigrants, ending with an aboriginal dance to protect the Games. It was a fabulous show, with Cathy Freeman, an aboriginal Australian, favoured to win gold in the 400-metre sprint, lighting the Olympic cauldron, followed by a fireworks display—or so I was told later.

I participated in the parade of the athletes around the track, but when we were shepherded into the centre of the stadium, where we were expected to stand for the ceremony, I was so sick I slumped to the ground. Eric knelt beside me. "Don't worry, Clara, just stay there. I'll stand over you so you won't get trampled." I slept in the midst of the din, in this great gathering of people—a speck on the ground, a small weak thing surrounded by the world's greatest athletes, watched by thousands in the stands and millions more on TV.

In the lead-up to our races, Lyne Bessette and I rose early one morning to check on the progress of our former Saturn teammate, Nicole Reinhart, who was in Arlington, near Boston, competing in the 2000 BMC Software Cycling Grand Prix. It was the fourth and last race in a series that offered any rider who won all four a grand prize of $250,000. Nicole had only to win this last race and the prize would be hers. She was a vivacious young woman, who had wanted more than anything to make the American Olympic cycling team. She'd been devastated when she fell short, but we told her not to worry. It wasn't her time. She'd get there eventually.

On the morning of September 18, three days after the Sydney Opening Ceremony, I checked my laptop for news of Nicole's race the previous day. I stared at the headline: TRAGEDY IN BOSTON.

Lyne, who'd come up behind me, screamed.

Nicole was dead.

I stood in disbelief, then escaped to the bathroom.

Later, Dede Barry, who had ridden with Nicole that day, would recount the story behind that ghastly headline: "We were in the final kilometres, with everything unfolding perfectly. The team was acting as *domestiques* for Nicole, trying to keep the field together, setting things up to give her the best chance to win. I pulled up the final hill behind Nicole, and we began our descent, three kilometres from the finish on a straight path. There was a dip in the road that we couldn't see because of the shadows from the trees. Somehow, Nicole's foot and left pedal hit the curb, and she lost control. She sailed into the air, struck a tree, then bounced to the ground. We all stopped. She lay there, unmoving, as the paramedics arrived. A few minutes later, her parents and her boyfriend, who'd come to watch, ran up the hill toward us. We took Nicole to the hospital, where she was pronounced dead."

All of us were in severe shock—Dede at the scene, Lyne and I, and Nicole's other teammates, here in Sydney representing their various countries, a day later. As well as grieving for a beloved teammate, we were forced to face our own mortality and recognize the preciousness of life—and how short it might prove to be.

Nicole's death limited the risk Dede, Lyne, and I were willing to undergo from then on. Dede never recovered her novice's nerve, even after taking two years off. Lyne froze in the midst of the Tour de l'Aude a few years later, then decided she was finished. I, too, would leave cycling.

But all that was to come. For now, Lyne and I were in Sydney, with the Olympics before us. I had thought the Games were the most important event in my life, but was I ever wrong. As I stared at my reflection in the bathroom mirror, I said to myself: *Who do you think you are, feeling sorry for yourself because you're not feeling well? If you can't race for yourself, do it for Nicole, who died doing something she loved.*

The next day Lyne and I put on black arm bands. I had come to

Sydney hoping to improve on my two Atlanta bronze medals. Now I didn't care how I placed, so long as I gave racing everything I had so that I could at least finish.

The road race was nine days after Nicole's death. The weather was horrible, with rain pouring from a black sky. When Geneviève Jeanson had a flat, I slowed while her wheel was changed, then let her draft behind me back to the pack. Since she was riding well, and I felt sick, I thought the least I could do was to help the team. After that, I kept falling back until I was fifteen minutes behind. Everyone was dropping out. Ina Teutenberg called over. *"Shiza!"* she cursed. "This sucks. You should quit and save it for the time trial."

I told her, "It's the Olympics. We can't quit."

She stopped anyway, then went to the cabanas, where warm tea and dry towels awaited, but I kept telling myself: *I'm finishing.*

When I turned into the stretch, people cheered in sympathy, because I was all alone—a pathetic, wet, sick figure, pedalling away, with every revolution of the wheel becoming harder and more resistant. On the scoreboard, I saw the number 23, which meant the main peloton had passed twenty-three minutes ago.

Finally, the rain stopped, the air grew misty, and the low clouds parted. I arrived at Centennial Park with 3 kilometres to go, and so far behind the peloton that volunteers were pulling down the barricades as if the race was over. One guy stopped to shout at me, "Hey, Canada! Finish with your head held high!"

That volunteer made me smile for the entire last lap, which was the kindest thing anyone could do.

At the finish line, everyone was celebrating, because someone had won. I wove through the crowd to greet the media scrum, having finished forty-third of forty-nine. When journalists asked about the race, I said, "I'm here to compete for Nicole. My victory was in not quitting, and I'm proud of what I've done."

The time trials were four days later. Every morning, I woke up to find my roommate, Tanya Dubnicoff, who'd already finished racing, coming home from an all-night party. We'd have breakfast together and we'd talk. Since I felt horrible about Nicole's death and was still physically ill, Tanya's presence helped a lot. Even though she was a sprinter, she rode with me and did my practice intervals, yelling: "C'mon, Clara, you can do it!" Between Tanya and a massage therapist—a huge, rough Jamaican dude, whose treatments made me feel almost like I was being beaten—I felt okay going into the event.

On the morning of the time trial, I found that somebody had left my turbo trainer—a stationary practice bike—in the Athletes' Village. Tanya offered to get it but was stopped by the cops for speeding—more or less rally-car driving. While I waited, Eric made me ride the course once, then a second time—something I would not have done if the turbo trainer had been there. Suddenly, I started to feel a bit better. After returning to the site, Tanya stood by me as I hammered away on the turbo trainer.

Early in the race, I found myself going full out, and I thought: *I'm having the kind of day Eric told me about.* On the second lap—about halfway through—I passed the Swiss rider who'd started a full two minutes in front of me. I was flying, just moving, moving, moving. Sensing me at her side, the Swiss rider pushed harder, and in that instant I lost my zone, worrying more about her than focusing. I started to hurt a little and then I lost my rhythm.

At the end of the race, Eric said, "You had the kind of amazing day you're capable of. It was fantastic to watch. If only you hadn't worried about the other rider and just run your own race."

Still, I had been good, very good. I ended up twenty seconds off the podium, in sixth place, but I felt awesome, considering how far I'd come after being down so long. The race hadn't been about coming first, second, or sixth. It was about a new kind of training that helped me know myself better as a person and as an athlete. Always before, my vision of excellence had had me on the podium, not standing in the crowd watching the medal ceremony. All that had changed.

Because I hadn't won, I was free to do whatever I wanted. Tanya suggested, "Hey, do you want to go surfing at Bondi Beach?"

Since we couldn't find a taxi or a bus, we stuck out our thumbs, two hosers trying to get a lift. A car stopped. A woman and a man told us to hop in, then drove us forty-five minutes out of their way to the beach, feeling excited to be connected to the Olympics in some way.

At Bondi, Tanya and I surfed all day. Ina Teutenberg met us, and it was perfect.

On my post-Olympic return flight to Canada, the pilots invited me into the cockpit. An attendant announced that I was on the plane, and everyone cheered, even though I hadn't won anything. I felt great, cruising through the skies on my way to Winnipeg. I couldn't help contrasting this with my glum mood after Atlanta, when I'd returned with two medals. It confirmed that how I felt depended on whether I accepted myself, and how I defined success and failure.

Since 1990, riding had been my job, my way of life. I'd worn the yellow jersey in the Tour Cycliste Féminin; won the biggest races in North America; earned a silver medal in the 1995 World Championships; won two bronze medals in the 1996 Atlanta Olympics, and earned a spot on the world's best women's professional cycling team.

On the flip side, the scars on my body told another story: being slammed into guardrails at 70 miles per hour; crashing on a headfirst descent and receiving a 3-centimetre gash under my left eye; another scar on my shoulder so big and ugly that kids often asked if it was bubble gum.

In peak years, I'd ridden nearly 23,000 kilometres, more than most people drive. But cycling had also put my first dream—to skate in the Winter Olympics—on hold.

I'd been brooding about this since before the Sydney Games, resulting in periods of quiet and irritation that Peter had begun to notice. Months before, when he'd asked me during a hike what was wrong, I had answered honestly, both for Peter and for myself: "I'm not sure I'm following the right path. I keep asking myself if I'm ever going to skate again."

My mom had sent me a VHS tape of all the speed-skating races in the 1998 Nagano Olympics, which I'd watched over and over again.

They made me yearn to know how good I could be, racing against the Germans, the Dutch, and all the other world champions.

When I shared these thoughts with Peter, his advice was encouraging, as always. "What's to stop you from finding out? Why not spend a week skating at the Calgary Oval? Either you'll get skating out of your system, or you can decide to go back to it full-time after the Sydney Olympics."

I followed Peter's advice.

I had my week of ice skating in Calgary, and I loved it.

On my arrival home from the Sydney Olympics, when Winnipeg reporters asked me about my future, I looked each one squarely in the eye, and I replied: "I'm going back to speed skating."

SKATES
2000–2010

12

LIVING THE DREAM

I remember in 1993, I rode in my first World Championship in Hamar, Norway. A temporary cycling track had been built in the magnificent Viking Ship oval, designed as the speed-skating venue for the upcoming 1994 Winter Olympics.

As I took my place at the start line for the individual pursuit, the announcer called out, "And now we have Clara *Huge* from Canada."

It was funny, and it pissed me off, and I didn't win anything in Norway that year. Nevertheless, what made the event so special was standing in the entrance of the Viking Ship oval, staring into its soaring heights, and thinking: *One day I'll be back here as a speed skater.*

I don't know what convinced me of this. Maybe it was the same sort of foresight that I'd experienced when I watched Gaétan Boucher float over the ice at the 1988 Calgary Olympics.

I don't believe in destiny, any more than I believe that if you wait long enough your true calling will find you. I believe we create opportunities that we follow or we don't. I've always felt I was meant to skate well, and that I would find some way to make this happen. I cycled because that opportunity presented itself when I needed it, and I found I was good at it. I'm grateful that cycling came first, because it prepared me to approach skating with the same determined endurance.

Three weeks after the Sydney Olympics, I sublet a room in the house of my old cycling teammate Tanya Dubnicoff near Calgary's Olympic Oval, where I planned to train as a speed skater. The oval attracted skaters from all over the world—Russia, Korea, China, Japan, Germany, France, everywhere. It was quite a spectacle to see so many of the best flying around the 400-metre oval at breakneck speeds.

It was a major transition for me to move from summer to winter, from bicycle to blades, from concrete to ice. My speed-skating experience had spanned two seasons when I was sixteen and seventeen, so now I was essentially a novice at the ripe old age of twenty-eight.

In cycling, I had become accustomed to being supplied with all my equipment, so when I had to buy new $1400 skates, I was in shock. These featured "klap" technology, a Dutch innovation that enabled the blade to detach at the heel. A spring-loaded hinge under the ball of the foot snapped the blade back into position after each stroke. By allowing greater pressure to be applied through the calves, the high-tempered steel blade remained in contact with the ice for longer, maximizing output for energy invested.

Going from being paid to race to paying to train seemed like a serious downgrade, but I was so psyched that it didn't matter. I paid my oval fees, I paid my coaching fees, I squeezed into my drab, faded turquoise Manitoba skin suit, with its sleeves reaching mid-forearm and its legs mid-calf. A couple of friends had offered me their Team Canada skin suits, but I wanted to earn mine.

Speed skating was calm and predictable compared to the chaos of road cycling, yet much more technically challenging. My schedule called for me to train six days a week—stretching and warm-ups, technique and racing, weight training, running, and riding on a stationary bike. My first week on the ice gave me tendinitis. Speed-skate boots are supposed to mould to the feet, with the heel reinforced for extra stability, and I had yet to develop the calluses and bone spurs of the seasoned skater.

More misery: My body was unprepared for the torturous posture—bent forward from the waist to reduce air resistance, one arm folded across the back, the other swinging. The lower the crouch, the more the legs could extend sideways during the push, lengthening the time spent applying force to the ice before the klap's rhythmic snap back into place.

The year before, when I had spent a week testing my desire to return to skating, Jacques Thibault, the oval's general manager, had encouraged me; however, after I arrived, he enrolled me in a program that I thought was weak, leaving me frustrated and unfulfilled.

Having been trained to cycle by a coach from the Eastern Bloc, I wanted to work harder than the program I was offered. I was seriously considering moving to Holland to be with the world's skating elite when Olympic medalist Susan Auch had a sudden inspiration: "Why not train with Xiuli Wang?"

Though Xiuli Wang was only an entry-level coach, Susan insisted her skaters were technically very good.

Xiuli had been China's first-ever World Championship medalist in women's speed skating, having won gold in 1990. Because she was overtrained as part of the Chinese sports machine, she had blown out her knees multiple times by her early twenties. After studying English on a scholarship in Ottawa, she was hired in Calgary for the oval, despite her still-limited language skills. Jacques Thibault encouraged her to become certified under the national coaching program, and she easily completed two years in one.

When I tested the idea of working with Xiuli on Jacques, he described it as "crazy but brilliant—an Olympic medalist slumming with athletes who will probably never get close to the Games."

Fine. I knew I didn't need the spur of other skaters with more miles in their legs to push me to excel.

Xiuli, then age thirty-six, had no idea who I was. All she knew was that I had built up endurance while cycling, and that I was used to distance training. We connected because she liked my work ethic and my willingness to take risks. I liked her bluntness, her demanding attitude, her dedication, her relentless push for perfection—all qualities that scared off many other skaters.

Seven weeks after starting with Xiuli, I raced in the national team trials. Amazingly, I was on pace to skate the Canadian 3000-metre record when I fell with only 100 metres to go, then climbed up, went the wrong way, turned around, and, yes, finished, having missed the standard for the World Cup team. The organizers said I could re-skate in forty-five minutes.

I was enthusiastic. Though many skaters and coaches thought I was foolish to try to race twice in such a short time, this was something I was used to doing as a cyclist.

Xiuli agreed: "Let's do it!"

This time, I made the team standard by three-tenths of a second. Everyone was surprised. In seven weeks, I had earned my Canadian racing skin suit.

I was now expected to train with the national team, but I said, "No, I'm staying with Xiuli." After years of being told what to do and how to train—of being manipulated and controlled—I wanted to set my own course. I knew what I needed, where I wanted to go, and how to get there. I also knew that I had a coach whose intensity matched my own.

Since Xiuli had assumed I would train with the national team, she was surprised when I declared my loyalty to her. Our bond was cemented. She had found her student. I had found my teacher.

Despite my training outside the national team system, I was expected to report to our team physiologist, Dr. David Smith. Though he would eventually earn my respect, at first he pissed me off, much like my coach Eric did before I realized his brilliance. Doc Smith was all about the numbers. He loved to have us in his lab, where he could measure our body composition and test our strength. My first body comp results, indicating that I was 21 percent body fat, carried Doc Smith's pencilled notation "Could improve." I thought: *Fuck you, man. You're not going to turn skating into cycling for me.* I was determined that my feedback would be on the ice—my lap times, my race results.

The international speed-skating season consists of six to eight World Cup events, followed by two World Championships. The World Cup at Heerenveen in the Netherlands, centre of the speed-skating universe, would be my first test against an international field.

Since I knew none of the skaters on the circuit, I studied them, becoming intimate with their times, how they warmed up, how they raced. Speed skating, like cycling, involves a great deal of strategy—whether you lead or conserve your energy, whether you throw in sprints along the way or save up for the finish. Passing a competitor requires acceleration and agility, with the overtaking skater responsible for any mishaps or illegal obstructions.

I had the audacity to believe I could beat them all, maybe not immediately, but in time. I just had to learn how to skate first.

Because training times on the Thialf oval were not yet available, a few of us began practising among the skating public. There we were, in the midst of an outdoor carnival, trying to do our intervals, surrounded by three hundred local people. When I swooped around one turn, I found a little girl standing in my way. Though I tried to swerve by her, I nailed the poor thing. After I told her how sorry I was, she asked if I was on the Canadian team. When I replied that I was, a smile changed her face. Canadians are still very popular in Holland, because they had helped liberate the Dutch during World War II. I was just glad I hadn't killed her.

Before my first event, I extended my arm to the attendant to receive my racing band. He laughed. "That's the wrong arm. Your first race?"

I was placed in the last pair of the B Group, and because I was racing with a Dutch skater, the rink was packed with ten thousand fans cheering for Holland. The energy was insane, so I imagined the cheers were for me. I skated my ass off and won the B Group.

Coming down the backstretch, I had noticed a small figure near the sidelines: the little girl I'd hit on the public rink. She held up a paper and pen, so I crouched down and signed my name—my first autograph as a speed skater.

After I moved into the A Group, all my teammates talked about was how great the Germans were. I told them, "They're not exceptional beings. They win and lose like everyone else."

Because of my philosophy, I went full out in every race. Experts told me, "Clara, you've got to skate to particular lap times," but I just shook my head. To me, if you're skating to lap times, you'll never know how hard you could have gone. I started as fast as I could, and I ended as fast as I could, and I blew up hard in almost every race. Nevertheless, once I qualified in the A Group, I stayed there. Playing safe was never part of my plan.

My second World Cup was in the Viking Ship in Hamar, Norway, so here I was, just as I had predicted as a cyclist back in 1993, entering that huge oval resembling an overturned boat hull. I didn't win any medals, but Peter Mueller, the legendary speed-skating coach—a rough, burly type of guy—told me that he'd brought one of his skaters to watch me race. He wanted to show him how "just to go for it." Mueller also told me that if I kept doing what I was doing, eventually I would break through. I took his words to heart.

I had had a momentous first skating season, living my dream. The next big challenge? My first Winter Games, in Salt Lake City in 2002.

13

THE WEDDING BIRD

When I was training for the Sydney Olympics, I fell in love with Glen Sutton, a village nestled in a bucolic river valley in Quebec's Eastern Townships. During the summer of 2000, while Peter was on another bike tour, this time through Quebec, Labrador, Newfoundland, and Nova Scotia, I decided to buy our first house there.

In my instructions to our real estate agent, I had stressed location. I wanted a property accessible only by one small mountain road, which turned into a smaller road, which turned into a dirt road, which turned into an even smaller dirt road, which turned into a forest, where I could not easily be found. When our agent came up with exactly what I had requested, while Peter was still out of touch on his bike tour, I bought it anyway.

Peter was surprised on his return: "You mean you just made this decision without asking me?"

Coexisting was still something I was learning, but I knew Peter would love the place, and he did. Besides its wooded hills, perfect for hiking and biking and camping, both of us were intrigued by rural Quebec, its culture and history. People wore their hearts on their sleeves, were passionate about food, and had strong family ties. Peter, in particular, felt an immediate kinship because of similarities to his Latino culture.

Three weeks after we had taken possession, I had to move to Calgary to train with Xiuli. Meanwhile, Peter hiked the northern section of the Appalachian Trail from Maine to the Hudson River during extreme weather, stopping only to watch my races. That winter, our life together—but mainly apart—began to take an emotional toll on me. During our five-year partnership, we'd spent most of our time in different places, different countries. This was especially true now, with me based in Calgary and Peter based in Glen Sutton. Too many significant thoughts, emotions, and events—like my purchasing of the house—had been unshared. Despite our letters, e-mails, and phone calls, I began to feel we had drifted apart and were now out of whack. As I brooded throughout my first skating season, I came to a troubling emotional place. I didn't know if I wanted to commit to anyone—not even to Peter.

Did I need a partner? Were we even a "couple" anymore? Perhaps the closeness we once possessed was now over. If so, shouldn't we acknowledge that?

For me, there had never been any thought of a "next step." I was devoutly anti-marriage, given the lack of positive role models on both sides of my family. Neither Peter nor I wanted to have children. Though I was curious about them and felt much in common with those who'd led difficult lives, I had no desire to further complicate my world. Our lifestyle hadn't even allowed for owning a houseplant, let alone a pet, which I'm allergic to anyway.

The "future" was not something Peter and I had felt much urge to discuss. He had always seemed okay with our relationship, however it evolved, and I had also liked things well enough as they were. We had experienced our ups and downs, not only because of the tensions created by my career but also because of my insecurities. Without question, my depression, still unacknowledged, played a serious role. No matter what we did together, I had few moments in which I could feel completely "present" the way Peter could. That was a sensation I experienced only when pushed to my limits, like while racing, or when challenged by a mountain. During quiet times, I was always battling an internal darkness, making me impatient and intolerant, very much like my dad. It was frustrating for Peter when I responded to his compliments as negatively as to any hint of criticism. He would ask, "What's going on? Where is this coming from?" Since I didn't know, I couldn't tell him, and his reasonable questions only annoyed me.

Sometimes I would have screaming fits. Something small would trigger me, and I would yell, seething with fury—once again just like Dad. I knew my reaction was over-the-top, but my unprovoked anger needed an outlet, so I kept finding ways to perpetuate it, even though that led to remorse.

Peter would walk away, saying, "I'm not going to argue with you when you're like this."

That sane response made me even angrier.

Since I could no longer hold bike racing responsible for my restless discontent, it was necessary to find something or someone to blame. Who else but Peter?

One day while I was in Calgary I phoned him in Glen Sutton to say, "You know, I'm not sure if I want to do this anymore."

"Do what?"

"Be a couple."

He was flabbergasted. "What do you mean?"

When I tried to explain, Peter became very upset in a way that surprised me.

"What's the big deal?" I asked him.

He replied, "Clara, I love you. And you're telling me you're not sure you want to be with me?"

Until that moment, I didn't realize how committed Peter was to our relationship. He had always given me the emotional space he thought I needed. All of a sudden, it hit me: *Man, what am I doing? I love him, too. We love each other!*

This exchange woke me up. I realized I would never find another person—this quality human being—who would care for me the way Peter did. I also saw that it was okay to love someone so strongly that you wanted to commit, and that this didn't have to end in failure. It was okay to honour our deep connection, and to work every day to strengthen and uphold it.

In spring, I returned to our Glen Sutton house, nestled in a forest above a gentle river valley. I returned to falling asleep in darkness and awakening to a flood of natural light, to the silence of nature, to sweet maple trees dripping with sap. I returned to Peter.

One day, as we were sitting on our couch, drinking delicious espresso, quietly talking, I suddenly heard myself ask, "What do you think about our getting married?"

Peter replied in surprise, "Clara, I've always wanted to be married to you."

We took a walk through the leafy hills behind our property, and that's when a wonderful thing happened. We saw a wood thrush for the first time in our forest. We'd often heard its flutelike song, echoing around us, on a summer's evening when the weather was cooling, but we had never seen the bird. Since we had binoculars, we watched our bird sing, and *oh, it was so rapturous!* That wood thrush became our wedding bird, and today, whenever I hear one, I return to that magical moment in the forest.

Peter and I had moved through our crisis. We loved each other, we shared the same values, and now we wanted to commit to staying together.

Neither of us knew how to make this happen. When I checked the Internet, I found that a Quebec civil ceremony required us to contact our local Palais de Justice (courthouse) for an interview. The nearest one was in the town of Cowansville.

Our interviewer made it clear that because we weren't religious, our marriage was a contractual agreement, with a two-and-a-half-week waiting period. When we asked why, we were told that was simply the rule.

We set the date for July 14, and then I called my mom and my dad. They didn't mind not attending our nuptials—in fact, I think my mom was relieved that she wouldn't have to manage my dad. Peter's mom and dad were probably disappointed not to be invited, but we just did not want to plan a complicated wedding.

About a week before the ceremony, Peter asked me, "What are you going to wear?"

"I don't know," I told him. I picked an unworn flowered skirt from my closet, along with a beige sleeveless linen blouse. "What about this?"

"Yeah. That's nice."

Peter took khaki pants and a button-down shirt from his closet. "Sure. That's good."

We just wanted to *be* married. We didn't care how it happened, as long as it wasn't one of those big, fussy events that blew up in your face.

Then, the day before our wedding, Peter wondered aloud, "So, should we get some rings?"

"I guess so."

Because I had interviews that would take all day, Peter made his way to the nearest Walmart, where he bought two gold bands. Yes, that's where we got our rings—we had no time to look anywhere else.

On July 14, we went to the courthouse, which had all the charm of a hardware store. My witness was my cycling coach, Eric Van den Eynde; Peter's was his University of Massachusetts roommate, Steve Anderson. The justice of the peace took us into a really ugly turquoise room, and since her English wasn't very good, she rushed through the vows.

She asked, "Do you have the rings?"

Peter searched his pockets until he found them, with both of us laughing.

"I now pronounce you man and wife."

The whole ceremony lasted two minutes and thirty seconds, as our photos with a background clock testify. We had photos only because we'd previously invited two friends from Montreal for the weekend, so we stuck to that plan, without telling them we were getting married.

Afterward, our wedding party returned to our house, where we drank champagne with our neighbours. Peter and I then walked through the leafy hills behind our property, where we'd heard our wedding bird sing. Later, we cut our wedding cake. I had baked it myself—carrot with cream-cheese frosting, decorated with flowers from our yard.

My most important wedding gift came at the end of the summer, when Peter joined me in subletting a Calgary apartment for the winter—a sacrifice for him, which drew us closer. This taught me what I should have already known. If I needed Peter, all I had to do was ask, and he'd drop whatever he was doing to come.

The Rockies, visible on a clear day 100 kilometres away, were a tease to both of us, reminding us of the Sierras and spurring a deep longing to climb those granite peaks. We were also grateful for the view of the shallow, clear waters of the Elbow River, flowing below our window.

We had gone from the sweet hum of birdsong, the rustle of the wind through maples turning scarlet, and precious moments of silence to the incessant hum of the urban engine—traffic, horns, sirens, planes. In Glen Sutton, even the rumble of our refrigerator had annoyed us. In Calgary, we hardly noticed it amid the metallic and electronic cacophony, which I referred to as "life in the Big Shitty."

As I prepared for the 2002 Games in Salt Lake City, Peter signed up for adult classes in French and writing at the University of Calgary. Sometimes he would run for three or four hours, and one day his eyelashes nearly froze shut while he was walking 20 kilometres to the oval to watch me race. He was literally passing time in the city, which he hated, without letting me know how much.

In 2004–5, Peter worked at Canada Olympic Park on an ice maintenance crew for the bobsled/luge track and otherwise made the best of another winter. He did have broad windows of adventure, like kayaking for three months in 2006 from the San Juan Islands in Washington to Skagway, Alaska, along the Inside Passage. I knew he needed to be by himself sometimes, and I liked the fact that he went, so we found a balance where we could support each other's interests while spending more time together.

Whenever I felt stressed or confused, I'd remember the two massive rocks in our Glen Sutton backyard, where I loved to lie down, gazing up into the leaves flowing over the branches of the maples and the birches, filling me with peace. It remains the quiet place to which I return when I need to calm down, travelling with me wherever I go.

Now, I was really living my dream . . .

14

SALT LAKE CITY OLYMPICS 2002

Compared with the Summer Games, the Winter Olympics are small and intimate. With 2399 athletes (instead of 10,000) representing 78 countries, competing in seven sports, Salt Lake City felt more like a festival than an enormous global phenomenon.

I was staying with other skaters in a condo in Kearns, Utah, a community in Salt Lake County that had begun life as a World War II army air base. Now it was a bona fide 'hood with a strong immigrant population, along with Latino and Mexican supermarkets. It was very rough, with regular shootings, but I liked its electric atmosphere better than the Athletes' Village.

Since the torch relay was passing right by our condo, I asked my roommates if anyone was going to watch. They were either too blasé, or too anxious about their events, or too uptight about the neighbourhood to leave our nest, so I went by myself, standing patiently at curbside with the crowd.

As soon as the torch came into view, everyone cheered, including me. It had already travelled over 13,500 miles, carried by more than 12,000 bearers, and it was beautiful—a rising flame, bouncing across our heads, with the poetry of the moment bringing tears to my eyes. This was the kind of purity I'd been hoping for since 1988, when Gaétan Boucher's performance had captured my imagination. Then, as now, I was seeing the importance of the Olympics from the perspective of someone watching it, rather than someone with the pressure of competing in it.

I returned to our condo with my face hidden in the shadow of my jacket collar, feeling a little embarrassed about having become so emotional. Besides, this moment belonged to me, only me. I wanted to hold on to it until the instant I stepped onto the rink.

The Opening Ceremony was also deeply moving. I watched along with a stadium crowd of 50,000, plus more than 2 billion TV viewers, as an honour guard of American athletes, flanked by New York City firefighters and police officers, carried a flag rescued from the World Trade Center after it was destroyed. The theme of the ceremony was Light the Fire Within, and for the first time, Utah's five Native American tribes appeared together, entering the stadium on horseback, then performing a vibrant stomp dance. Against the red and golden beauty of the Utah landscape, giant puppets of local animals were brought to the ice. They reminded me of the puppet shows about Inuit mythology, performed with sealskin dolls, that my dad had taken my sister and me to see at the Winnipeg Art Gallery. I also remembered visits to the studio of the First Nations artist Jackson Beardy. He'd given me a little leather medicine turtle, which I had carried all over the world with me. I thought about my First Nations friends in Elmwood and wondered what had become of them, after such a rough start to their lives.

The Native American theme resonated with me, especially after I heard Native American drumming described as the heartbeat of the earth.

As for the Games themselves, I was bursting at the seams with energy. Normally the better I felt, the higher my confidence. This was different. Peter, who had travelled to the Games with me, lamented, "I've never seen you so nervous before a race." I couldn't eat. I was in full-panic mode.

Xiuli patiently reminded me that I'd been on the ice for only one season, in contrast to the years I'd spent building up my experience in cycling. To be at this level so suddenly was absurd.

She was right. I still had days when I exclaimed to myself in disbelief: *I can skate—I can really skate!*

Slowly, confidence replaced fear as I began to rediscover my rhythm—that feeling of floating above the ice with ease, completely relaxed and fluid. Though this was my third Olympics, it was the first in which I felt able to enjoy myself doing something I loved.

The day of my 3000-metre race, I rode my bike to the venue, went through security, then did my warm-up in an empty rink. I worked the stationary bike and stretched, feeling alone among the other athletes. Though Cindy Klassen, Kristina Groves, and I were all racing for Canada, we were deeply competitive, even if no one admitted it. We didn't wish each other bad luck, but we were with our own coaches, focused on our own programs. The fact that Xiuli wasn't working with "elite" skaters also created separation between us.

After coming off the ice, I did my warm-down, rested in the dressing room, then studied my schedule, working backward from my start time, which was 2:43 P.M. I had also given copies to Xiuli, my skate technician, and my massage therapist, instructing them to contact me only if a natural disaster wiped out the Games.

I did my final warm-up on the bike—twenty minutes subaerobic, three minutes on, two minutes off; two minutes on, one minute off; one minute on, then thirty seconds off. I followed this with a few sprints, three more minutes of subaerobic, then a cooldown with some final stretching. I put on my skin suit, collected my skate bag, jacket, and warm-up pants, then went up through the tunnel to the infield, feeling completely inside myself, determined, and ready to go.

All that changed the moment I arrived at the infield. An American skater was halfway through her 3000-metre race in a stadium bursting with electricity and energy. Despite my Olympic experience, I felt overwhelmed, standing at the heart of this great and terrifying swirl, afraid I might break down. As I closed my eyes, instructing myself to breathe and go to a safer place, I suddenly remembered Jackson Beardy's little leather medicine turtle, tucked in my bag. I held it in my hands—a spirit totem, symbolizing the wisdom of the earth, telling me that I was exactly where I needed to be at this moment.

By then, Xiuli was at my side, looking concerned. She told me to take a few more deep breaths. Though I could barely speak, I assured her, "I'm okay."

The start line. The gun. The race . . .

I placed a respectable ninth in an event that saw a world record broken. Cindy Klassen won bronze, Canada's first medal of the Games. I had told Eric Van den Eynde, "If I finish in the top ten in the 3000 metres, I'll win a medal in the 5000."

I was now in a position to test that assertion.

My race was the last speed-skating event of the Games, so I had a lot of time to put in. I remember sitting at a table in the Athletes' Village with the U.S. women's hockey team, watching the Canadian women's hockey team struggle against the Swedes. The Americans were laughing at our team, calling them losers. Their dissing never stopped, till Canadian figure skater Jamie Salé finally told them: "Just watch, Canada is going to kick your ass!"

It was obvious that the Americans were far too cocky, and as it turned out, the Canadian women's team did beat these boastful women, winning gold. Our men's hockey team did the same to the American men, for another gold. Jamie and her partner, David Pelletier, also aced the figure-skating pairs competition, though this was not acknowledged until after the resolution of a judging scandal. Though our Canadians were clearly the best, the Russians were declared the winners. In the end, the two pairs shared gold.

As for my sport, speed skating was proving a disappointment for Canada. We had earned only two medals—Cindy Klassen's bronze in the 3000 metres and Catriona Le May Doan's gold in the 500 metres. Jeremy Wotherspoon of Red Deer, Alberta, considered one of the greatest sprinters of all time, and the favourite going into the Games, had fallen at the start of the 500 metres. Then he had finished only thirteenth in the 1000 metres. People were talking about this ad nauseam, which was hardly what I wanted to hear preparing for my event. I kept repeating to myself, *Listen, guys, that's too bad, but that was Jeremy, not me.*

By this point in the Games, most of the athletes and their coaches had completed their responsibilities. They and the staff were partying long and hard, but Xiuli kept me steady by insisting, "Just pay attention to yourself and what you came here to do."

Some guy shouted, in a slurred voice, "Hey, are you going to see the Tragically Hip tonight?"

I replied, "No, I have to race in two days."

He moaned, "Oh, too bad, because it's going to be a really good show."

Peter was the perfect companion for these events—self-contained, undemanding, and always positive. He reminded me, "Clara, it's all bullshit. You can see a band anytime. You can buy a ticket. Those other athletes don't have another chance, but you still do, so don't waste it."

Two nights before my race, I came back to the Kearns condo to find that everyone was off somewhere and I was locked out. It took me an hour to find the manager, by which time I was seething. After I finally got in, I reminded myself to let go of my anger. Then I realized I was sharing space with another teammate who had failed to achieve his Olympic goals and was now having a terrible breakdown. Why I was rooming with a man was beyond me, though that was beside the point at the moment. I was so worried he would harm himself that I called every person I knew who might help. Finally, I found a coach, who contacted his parents, and they moved the poor guy out with his stuff. It seemed that everyone at these Games was now a tourist but me.

I still had my war.

I'd brought a stack of books, including one Peter gave me called *Zen Mind, Beginner's Mind* by Shunryu Suzuki. One sentence stated: "In the beginner's mind there are many possibilities, but in the expert's there are few." I reminded myself that I was a beginner among experts; therefore I had nothing to lose, with all possibilities open to me. I closed the book, feeling as if I'd learned something essential about who I was at these Games.

On the Internet, I also found an e-mail from a Cree family Peter and I had visited in La Ronge, Saskatchewan. I vividly remembered running down a trail to the lake, with their three children—Sekwan, Takwagen, and Keewetin—bounding ahead like fawns through the woods. Their mother, Bonnie, had written to say she and her family were praying to the four directions—north, south, east, and west—for my success and well-being. I reread that e-mail several times, pondering its wisdom.

> *EKWA!!! CLARA,*
>   *It means NOW.*
>   *The kids, Tim and me are with you.*
>   *The kids and I will burn sweet grass and pray to the 4 directions and*
> *ask the creator for help to find more strength for you.*
>   *Or to smile at you.*

When I awoke the morning of my 5000-metre race, I was feeling anxious. At the oval, I nervously checked my skates. A few days before, a friend had handled them, compromising the klap mechanism. They had been fixed, though, and now they were fine.

I began a vigorous warm-up till Xiuli stopped me, saying, "Go easy."

She knew I possessed enormous energy, ready to be released, and she wanted me to hold back for the race. Only Xiuli would have understood this, which was why she was my coach.

Despite my anxiety, I felt pulsatingly alive—a bundle of strength, endurance, and life. I found a pen and wrote *EKWA* on my hand as a reminder.

Gretha Smit from Holland skated early and was phenomenal. When she crossed the finish line in first place, a guy from the Russian team held up his hands in front of my face as if to say: *Well, I guess it's over for you.*

I thought: *Oh no, it isn't. If she can do it, so can I.*

I received the "ready" call to head for the start line.

Because speed skating is a solo sport, the outcome rests solely with the athlete. As I waited, I peeled my suit from my hand, where I'd printed *EKWA,* and felt calmer.

The gun sounded, and I was off the line, ready to skate the race I had visualized for hundreds of hours, hitting the same pace I had in the 3000 metres—very fast. Very, very fast, without blowing up. I caught the edge of my skate with two laps to go, felt myself fumble, then pushed myself to attack even harder.

In the backstretch, I was consumed by pure, total pain, right to my core. I had never before hurt myself the way I did in that race. I went so far inside my reserves and my muscle fibres that I was in a toxic state. Coming across the finish line, I snowploughed, stumbled off the ice, then collapsed on the bench in a great, heavy *THWUMP*. I had severe muscle cramps and nausea. I thought I was having a heart attack, maybe an aneurysm, till I realized: *Clara, you just skated 6:53!*

I'd taken seven seconds off my personal best, and I was in second place. Xiuli massaged my legs, but the pain was still so bad that I cried uncontrollably, with all of that hurt spilling out of me.

I watched the next pairs. I was still in second, then Claudia Pechstein of Germany, who'd won gold in the 5000 metres during the last two Olympics, broke the world record, putting me in third. I was sure the last pair would beat me, but they faltered with three laps to go.

Xiuli exclaimed, "Clara, I think you did it!"

"No, *we* did it."

Afterward, I went to the Medal Plaza, where I stepped up onto the podium to receive my bronze medal—the only Canadian athlete ever to win medals at both Winter and Summer Olympic Games. In that moment, I thought about my first skating coach, Peter Williamson, who had died at such a young age. It was Peter who first believed in me, who saw in my youthful eagerness the raw beginnings of an athlete. When I'd skated here in Utah, I felt Peter's intensity in my heart, his competitive fire in my blood. When I'd told Xiuli that *we* had won, I was also seeing Peter Williamson's smiling face.

That night, Peter and I barely slept, and the next morning I had to ask, "Did that really happen, Pete?"

I took my medal from its bag and said with a kid's pride, "Look what I got!"

In fact, we both felt like kids—giddy and in a beautiful daze. Then, almost immediately, I became sick—relief, I suppose.

At the Closing Ceremony, I watched from the stands as KISS and Bon Jovi played, remembering how much I'd loved the latter band as an unruly teenager, and now here I was, watching them at the Olympics, where I'd won a medal.

I felt joyful.

I also thought about those other Olympians, like my roommate, whose failure to live up to some inner goal had driven them to the brink of despair. I knew that feeling, and I suspected that my medal might provide only temporary relief for problems that I had yet to face and conquer in a different arena.

My emotional victory was this: At least now—*EKWA!*—I was allowing myself to enjoy the moment.

15

ON TOP OF THE WORLD

For my Olympic service, Air Canada had given me two tickets to any-where in the world. My choice? The Far North for a delayed honey-moon.

Peter had talked a lot about the landscape around the Yukon Territory—the endless rivers and gorgeous terrain. I had longed to share that with him. We decided to cycle the Dempster Highway, seek-ing light, air, and space, and an openness of experience that my bubble of training could never provide.

The Dempster is a 737-kilometre, all-weather road running from Dawson City northeast across the Arctic Circle to Inuvik. Officially opened in 1979, it was named for RCMP Inspector William Dempster, whose dogsled runs had created the trail for much of the highway.

Though many people might be surprised at my choice of a "break" from training, exhaustion always makes me feel alive and satisfied. Peter feels the same. Our level of tolerance for physical activity is much higher than that of most everyone else. For me, movement through nature is pure medicine, for both body and mind.

Since Peter had already spent a month touring the Yukon and Alaska, I was to fly to Whitehorse, then meet him in Dawson City, once the centre of the Klondike gold rush. I would be abandoning my $18,000 time-trial bike for a self-assembled $150 touring bike, which was like downgrading from a Ferrari to a VW bus.

Though Peter often sought out dirt roads, I never liked them, as they usually meant a laborious slog over washboard, soft sand, rocks, and potholes. Yet we were lured to the adventures they offered.

After a few nights at the Dawson City River Hostel, we collected our gear—tent, stove, cook pot and Teflon pan, clothing, rain ponchos, sunglasses, bear spray, Swiss Army knife, headlamps, duct tape, tools, spare tubes, patch kit, and a bike pump. To this we added food: pasta, bread, pancake mix, sun-dried tomatoes, cookies, chocolate, tea, coffee, powdered milk, sugar, maple sugar, jam, peanut butter, olive oil, apples, and a cabbage (we chopped it up after three days, then ate it raw with olive oil, salt, pepper, and fresh lemon juice—delicious!). By the time we packed all this in our panniers, our bikes probably weighed about seventy-five pounds each. At 6:00 P.M. we set off, knowing we would have daylight till around 1:00 A.M.

That first evening was bike-touring bliss, like riding into the pages of a storybook, painted with the most delicate sunset shades, as we headed 40 kilometres east to the Dempster turnoff. The temperature cooled as the sun dipped behind the western peaks, with shadows masking their vibrant green. At a creek, we pulled over for pasta and tea. Warmer clothing came out of our packs as our breath began to show in the calm evening air. It was 11:00 P.M. before we saw an inviting camping spot along a stream.

After setting up the tent, we filled our water bag with icy mountain water, and I did my cold-water dance. Nothing calms me after a day of cycling like a cold rinse. It was a love-hate relationship I had developed with camp showers.

Early-morning light revealed a forest of aspen, willow, and spruce, rising up surrounding the summits. Low-bush cranberries, mushrooms, crowberry, lichen, mosses, kinnikinnick, and dwarf birch carpeted the spongy forest floor. This was my first real look at the diversity of northern flora, and what a spectacular array it was.

Travelling north, I glimpsed movement in one of the natural pools. I assumed it was something small like a duck or a beaver. As we drew closer, I was delighted to see a bulky moose gracefully taking its early-morning dip.

Just as icy rain began to fall, we reached the Tombstone Campground. Our haven was the screened-in picnic shelter with a barrel stove pumping out heat to warm our frozen extremities.

We hoped the rain would cease before we started up the North Fork Pass, the highest point of the Dempster at 4229 feet. No such luck. As we gained altitude, the rain intensified and the temperature dropped. A veil of dark grey clouds hid the distant Tombstone Mountains. I was disappointed to be putting on more rain gear instead of admiring the rugged northern range I had seen in photographs.

Patiently we crept up the steep grade, laden with food and camping gear, yet feeling grateful to be self-sufficient and ready for anything. Peaks came in and out of view, constant companions. Yet we were alone in that vast space of valley and mountains, with vehicle traffic deterred by the wet conditions. I thought about the original inhabitants of this land, the Gwich'in First Nation, living lives of sustenance, without vehicles or roads to deliver supplies. Even now, the land felt remote. I remembered a quote by Tr'ondëk Hwëch'in elder Percy Henry from the Tombstone Range guidebook, now running through my head like poetry: "You have everything you want there. There's all kinds of berries, fish and little animals that live in that country. I was born and raised in that country. That's my university."

At Two Moose Lake, we stopped for lunch—bagel sandwiches and cookies—while gazing out at the graceful waterfowl. Placards detailed First Nations history. This was a hunting ground for moose, but the tribes had not taken more than they needed and had never eaten near the lake, a sign of respect for the moose's territory, I would imagine.

For hours, we moved through the Blackstone Uplands, with the help of a welcome tailwind easing our pedalling through the mystical country. Cold rain fell as we rushed to pitch our tent. As I unpacked with my back to the river, Peter suggested I look behind me. He had seen a wolf, which had vanished into the encroaching dusk. I was sad to have missed this elusive creature and hoped for another chance as the gurgling river lulled us to sleep.

The next day we were in rain after twenty-five minutes. As we approached the Ogilvie Mountains, we saw a truck with a camper slow to a stop through the drizzly mist. A smiling face appeared at the window. The driver described the landscape ahead—the limestone cliffs shaped like fortresses with spruce trees on top. "They look like people watching down on you. It's more beautiful than the gospel and heaven put together." His reverential tone reflected his appreciation for the ancient land, while his last words—"Don't give up, just don't give up"—reflected how difficult he knew our journey could become.

It's possible to be comfortable in the rain when wearing proper gear. My poncho, though awkward when flapping in the wind, was sufficiently warm and well ventilated. After sailing down Windy Pass, Peter and I rode side by side, silently moving at a touring pace. Though rain distorted the distance, I was sure something was on the road ahead. As we approached, the mysterious form materialized: a grizzly. We stopped in our tracks, 200 metres away, not caring about the inevitable chill from not moving. After twenty minutes of shivering, we tentatively proceeded, pausing for one last look through our binoculars. Peter spotted it high on the hillside, its massive bulk moving with ease over the land.

We arrived dirty and wet at the Engineer Creek Campground, with its towering limestone cliffs. Our intended quick lunch in the screened-in picnic shelter turned into a six-hour stay. A German couple—Heiko and Ankje—offered us hot spiced red wine, mouth-watering chocolate truffles, friendly conversation, and laughter.

We pedaled into the late-day light at 8:30 P.M., satisfied and full, under sun showers. After twenty minutes, we spotted a shadowy creature, illuminated by the soft light of the hour, below us along the Ogilvie River. A wolf! With its long, lanky legs planted firmly and its head lowered, it was in its "start" position, ready to dash. When I made a call like that of a crying wolf, it paused to curiously check us out. As I continued this odd whine, the stare-down went on. Five minutes later, our wolf disappeared into the bush.

Ten kilometres farther, we came upon four gulls, furiously dive-bombing a bald eagle in a tree. The eagle remained perched on its branch, seemingly unimpressed.

When setting up camp, we were treated to the water acrobatics of a lone beaver, playing in the calm pool beside the river. Each slap of its tail drew our attention, and it seemed to be having a grand time performing for us, the tourists. We thought of all the travellers in cars whom we'd met, obsessed with road conditions and the weather, and their consistent question: "Seen any animals?" How could they expect that thrill when the roar of their engines could be heard by wildlife kilometres away?

The ominous hum of mosquitoes awoke us early. I screamed and scratched while breaking camp. How could Peter look so calm, preparing pancakes in that vicious mayhem? Down by the river, I cried out in frustration, wondering if I'd make it out alive. I left in a fury, simultaneously stuffing pancakes rolled with black currant jam into my mouth and pedalling.

Soon we began the arduous climb out of the Ogilvie River Valley, up into the Eagle Plains. We assumed *plains* meant "flat," but we could not have been more mistaken. The steep grade opened up spectacular vistas as we paralleled the Ogilvie range, spoiled for me by my fatigue. Each time we crested a difficult pitch, I saw another one ahead. After 32 kilometres, I cracked. Hungry and tired, I collapsed on the roadside and began eating maple sugar, desperate for something sweet to stop the thumping in my head. I had the "bonk," a diabetic-like state of low blood sugar typical of athletes who don't eat enough. I had no one to blame but myself for having devoured all our snack foods the previous day, not thinking of the miles ahead.

Peter found some water, then made pasta in a sheltered spot off the road. We feasted on sautéed onions—something I hadn't particularly liked until that day, when hunger made that eye-watering vegetable my favourite delicacy. We also had pasta with olive oil, sun-dried tomatoes, and Parmesan cheese, followed by more pancakes. I was so tired we stayed the night.

Rain fell intermittently, but the next day we were greeted with sunshine and a mild tailwind, confirming we made a good decision to stay the night before. Slowly I was learning that when travelling, it was best to follow the natural flow of events, instead of rushing to some destination.

The next 130 kilometres took us through the steep undulations of the Eagle Plains—a sea of spruce, stretching out to the horizon. We rested in what had been a burned-out area while feasting on wild blueberries that flourished by the roadside. We consumed handful after handful until our bellies ached, having gorged on empty stomachs. Before long, we were in the bush, paying for our gluttony.

Less than a kilometre later, we discovered we were not the only ones enjoying the bounty. Two black bears, within 100 metres, scavenged the bushes as we hesitantly rode by. Fortunately, they preferred berries to bike tourists.

Late in the day, we glimpsed the velvety smooth Richardson Mountains, glowing softly in the fading light. We made the final climb to the Eagle Plains gas station and hotel/campground, which advertised itself as a "one stop truck stop." We were now at the halfway point of the Dempster. After a meal, followed by a hot shower to clean the clog of Dempster dust from our pores, we set up camp.

Awaiting us at the front counter was the food box we had packed in Dawson, taking advantage of the free car-delivery service offered to bikers. Chocolate, mangoes, oranges, apples, and cheese were a few of the treats we'd savour.

It wasn't until 4:30 the next afternoon that we left. Squeaky clean and stuffed with BBQ chicken burgers, fries, and soup. Though it had rained all morning, the day was beginning to dry as a cold wind blew from the southeast. En route to the Arctic Circle, we spotted orange cloudberries by the side of the road and stopped to pick some of the meaty delicacy, careful not to overdose as we had on blueberries.

Cold easterly winds continued to bite our exposed skin at the Arctic Circle, latitude 66 degrees 33 minutes north, marked by an informational display and washrooms. After munching on chocolate bars, we rode hard once again to stop our deep shivers. As we raced toward warmth, a porcupine stumbled up the hill to the south, like a ball of fire glistening in the setting sun.

We had thought the Dempster's novelty would end, but each day provided exciting new versions of the northern landscape. Before the final push to Rock Creek Campground, we stopped for another snack—cranberries, almonds, and walnuts—while gazing into the mountains, taking it all in. This was when we noticed the silence. We stopped talking, and listened: silence of an unmatched quality, like the beauty of the landscape; deafening, lonely silence that drives the unsettled to speak, the sad to cry, the fearful to run. So rare in our world. We sat, listened, then moved on.

We pulled into camp with one goal: warmth. As we rode to the picnic shelter, we scoped abandoned sites for split wood, hoping in vain for something to start our barrel stove. An older couple in a van from B.C. offered us some, and now the picnic shelter seemed like a five-star hotel. We felt as if we were living large in the wild, with apple cinnamon pancakes and cherry preserves. It was past two in the afternoon when we set out. We hoped to reach Fort McPherson that evening.

Winds roared from the south. At first, we naïvely thought this push would make the ride easy. Instead, we struggled to stay on the road as the winds shifted to the side, with freezing rain biting our skin. As we rode through the Richardson Mountains and over the border to the Northwest Territories, the wind tore through our clothes and pushed us off the road, forcing us to fight to remain upright.

Miraculously, we made it up and over the pass, hoping the worst was over. Normally such a climb would be followed by a rewarding descent, but now we could see that the road sloped down with the same steepness it had climbed, and the wind was still howling behind us. This was dangerous.

Peter's poncho acted like a sail. The gusts forced him to skid sideways downhill, with one foot dragging, while his back wheel tried to overtake his front one. He fought against toppling as the wind intensified, determined to knock him down. As Peter stopped, awkwardly trying to remove his poncho, the same wind attacked me.

When the wind shifted to our left, it became too strong for us to pedal. We were stranded and damn cold. Because the road was a slick clay, the wind was actually blowing the bikes off as easily as if they were on ice. I tried to hold mine steady but kept skidding. As a truck heading south slowed to a stop, Peter struggled to hold down his bike while I fought the wind to reach the truck's lowering window. Inside the cab, a family of eight sat warm and cramped, eyes wide in disbelief as the driver asked, "Are you two okay? It's really bad up ahead."

I must have seemed a little crazy with adrenaline as I sputtered, through my frozen jaw, a broken account of the last 19 kilometres. They were concerned they might not make the pass with their vehicle, even though we'd made it on our bikes.

We needed to move to keep from freezing, but the closest we came to riding was throwing one leg over the top tube and clicking into one pedal before the wind prevented us from gaining another inch. Shivers turned to convulsions, and our stiffened mouths refused to make intelligible sounds. While retrieving my glove that had taken flight, we discovered a relatively sheltered gully. This glorified ditch would be our camp for the evening.

Under my wet poncho, I struggled to get into something dry. Peter valiantly prepared cup after cup of hot chocolate, noodles, and tea. After two hours, clouds continued to scud across the wintry sky. Our small supply of water had been used. Fortunately, Peter discovered glistening pools of runoff in the tundra, less than 50 metres from our camp.

It was comical trying to pitch our tent as it fought to sail away. Peter attached four boulders to each corner. After the poles were inserted, it was my job to sit inside and further stabilize the thin nylon structure. Even with more rocks inside, it still threatened to blow away.

Our food supplies, though, were stashed under small boulders away from us. Outside, the storm raged.

We spent the remainder of the night listening to the slapping of the rain. It was the kind of weather one might expect climbing mountains, not bike touring.

A light snow greeted us the next morning. The winds had died to a breeze while wet flakes continued to fall. Our plan was to break this makeshift camp and ride to the official campground 70 kilometres away, in hopes someone would have a fire going in the wood stove. Six hours later, that wish was not only granted but bettered.

When I went to the visitors' centre to pay our camp fee, I must have looked such a mess that Orrie, its host, not only declined my money but offered Peter and me a heated log cabin with a hot shower. It's rare to meet someone as helpful and understanding as Orrie, but when you do, hardships dissipate. Peter and I found it marvellous to believe that after two such challenging days, we would stay warm, clean, and safe for a whole night. It was like Christmas, and we were children staring wide-eyed at an imaginary Christmas tree. Our cabin's shelves were filled with food left by other tourists: tuna, granola bars, soup, nuts, dried fruit, Kraft Dinner. A note said, "Eat all you want, or it'll go to waste."

Sleep came easily in our warm loft, and blue skies (well, partly) greeted us in the morning. We were still exhausted from two tough days, so when Orrie offered us the cabin for another night, we quickly accepted. We lounged around, munching on crepes filled with cherry preserves and cream cheese, drinking coffee and chai spice tea.

Inside the visitors' centre, a fire burned warm and welcoming, and we read about Gwich'in culture, depicted in a rustic display assembled by the local elders. It was easy to hitch a ride into Fort McPherson, the first true northern community we were to encounter, to resupply. Its houses were made of wooden clapboard, each with a snow machine in the driveway, and with everything muddy from the town's dirt-road grid. Chained huskies howled from their doghouses. This was not your typical tourist destination, but the inhabitants had tried, so we read their placards recounting the Hudson's Bay Company history and more Gwich'in culture.

We planned on an early start to arrive in Tsiigehtchic, 65 kilometres north, in time to tour the town, but that didn't happen. We were ready to ride, but our bikes were not. Our gear shifters had stopped working, seizing up after the fine silt and mud had jammed them. I ruined mine trying to make it work. For an hour, Peter patiently tried to fix it, using an Allen key, pliers, Swiss Army knife, and duct tape. And it worked! Well, relatively. I had only four gears.

Both of our bikes were in bad shape as a result of this unseasonably wet August on the Dempster. The next 57 kilometres were like riding through clay. My muscles ached because of limited gearing, and my bike was camouflaged with caked mud. Stunted spruce trees covered the land. The odd knoll, rising in the distance, resembled a porcupine on full alert. Lakes popped into view around every corner.

By 8:45 P.M. we reached our destination: the Mackenzie River and the ferry to Tsiigehtchic. It was Sunday. Too late for a crossing. In winter, vehicles travel over an ice bridge, which is considered part of the Dempster. When the water is open, there's only the ferry.

We had to find a place to camp. When Peter asked George, the ferryman, for water, George invited us to spend the night in his tent alongside the river. We were grateful, since using it would make break-ing camp in the morning a breeze. It was a large tent with a mattress and a vestibule. We brewed tea inside, knowing the mosquitoes were thick outside. The setting sun tinted the few clouds there were every colour in the spectrum. The almost clear sky tempted us to stay awake, in hopes of seeing the aurora borealis, but by 1:00 A.M. it was still too bright, so we settled for faint glimmers of what we liked to believe were the northern lights.

The mercury read −5°C as we snuggled cozily into down-filled bags.

By morning, the inevitable clouds had moved in, warming the earth like an atmospheric blanket. The scent of fresh rain wafting over the trees to the river spelled trouble for us, the bike tourists. Hastily we stuffed our panniers, then rushed to the ferry. Four sandhill cranes squawked on the shore. One of the few mistakes we made on this trip was not stopping to take a good look at these large, exotic creatures. As the ferry swung out from the sandy shore, George, our benefactor, in-vited us into the ferry office for hot coffee.

High on a cliff, and dominated by a church spire, Tsiigehtchic is a picturesque town located at the confluence of the Mackenzie and Arc-tic Red Rivers. At its small grocery store/café, we met Charlie, another cyclist, removing mud from his overturned bike. Charlie was a good storyteller and a good listener, so we exchanged hardship tales, happy to know we'd survived the same cold, wind, rain, and mud. We made cheese sandwiches, which we heated in the store's microwave, one after another, followed by yogurt and bananas. We talked with locals and got a feel for the village, population of about 150. Though rough on the outside, its people were friendly the moment we broke the tension with a smile.

On a second ferry, across what in winter was another icy section of the Dempster, we met a bike tourist named Oli—a Spaniard from Majorca. We set off together, with Oli setting the pace, up the climb from the river, then over the hard, flat, mud-packed road, pushed by a tailwind, taking turns at the front. After forty clicks, Oli was tired, while Peter and I, still in a hammering mood, continued at a good clip.

Up the road, we saw the silhouette of an overturned bike with someone working on the rear wheel. It was Charlie, upset over a broken spoke.

"I'm close to hitching a ride to Inuvik," he exclaimed.

We encouraged him to stick with it, since he'd been riding for six weeks from Vancouver and was now so close to his goal. Then, as we ate lunch on the side of the road, Oli pulled up, looking rested. Soon we were off, all four of us, each at our own pace, with plans to meet at Caribou Creek Campground.

It began to rain, and our tailwind turned to a crosswind. Because the campground where the four of us regrouped provided no shelter, Peter and I decided to carry on with the hopes of a better campground up the road. The rain continued. The winds picked up, but we thrust forward, having decided to push through our shivers and fatigue to Inuvik, some 45 kilometres away. We stopped for peanut butter and jelly bagels, then continued into the freezing rain and headwind. For me it was the coldest, wettest, toughest ride. Yes, epic. We arrived at 11:00 P.M., covered in mud, frozen, exhausted, and relieved to be at a campground with showers, having just ridden 120-plus kilometres on the wet, muddy Dempster.

But all was not well. In the women's shower, I cried under the cold, biting spray, lips purple, with shivers running deeper than when I'd been exposed to the elements. Peter came out of the men's shower, smiling and toasty. I went straight in after him, where I soothed my deep chill under the hot water.

Later, as the two of us sat around a fire, we thought back over our entire Dempster trip, so difficult, but with the magnificent landscape, minimal traffic, and such friendly people. We agreed that no other road tour could come close to its wildness, with bears, wolves, and so many other animals, combined with so little development, so little trash, so little tourism. We also agreed that we wouldn't have done anything differently, except we still regretted rushing past those sandhill cranes.

Otherwise, it had been a perfect honeymoon.

16

FAME—ON A BUDGET

Being the only Canadian ever to win both Winter and Summer Olympic medals was a wonderful achievement. But here's the hard truth: After the Salt Lake City Games, I didn't have a single sponsor.

Canadian athletes are like starving artists. We're expected to find gratification in being allowed to ply our glamorous, self-fulfilling trade. The concept of amateur and professional in international sports is an archaic one. I was competing against athletes who, in countries like Germany and Holland, were earning millions of euros a year. Even my national teammate Catriona Le May Doan, represented by the same agency as I was, was doing just fine, but for whatever reason I wasn't seen as marketable.

Claude Chagnon, whose family owns the Canadian integrated telecommunications company Vidéotron, heard of my plight. He had started the Fondation d'athlète d'excellence du Québec, allowing Quebec athletes to pursue an education while receiving funding for sport. He suggested that I, as a Quebec resident, take a few classes in order to qualify. Hubert Lacroix, CEO of CBC/Radio Canada, and one of the foundation's donors, gave Claude Chagnon a ringing endorsement of me: "When I watched Clara race in the Salt Lake Games, I didn't know who she was. I saw that she'd calculated her efforts to precisely hit the finish line within the last inch of the last stretch, and then I watched as she died. I'd never before seen an athlete give so much. I wondered: 'Is she real? Did what I see really happen?' After Clara came to Montreal for the short track speed skating championships, I knew she was the person I thought she was. She was always thinking about giving back.

She was clear about her motives, both on and off the ice, and was, in my mind, the perfect athlete to support to realize all she could become."

I signed up for a few fine arts courses, and the foundation provided me with $30,000 worth of funding sponsorship. On the advice of my cycling coach, Eric Van den Eynde, I also kept racing the bike so that the extra prize money I earned from the second sport would help me stay afloat. After Salt Lake City, I qualified to compete for our national cycling team at the 2002 Commonwealth Games in Manchester, England. I won gold in Manchester at the time trial, as well as bronze in the points race on the track. This was less than six months after the Salt Lake City Winter Games, and just before I joined Peter on the Dempster Highway.

In September, following the Dempster, I returned for the 2002–3 skating season. While I was shuffling across the ice, standing straight up instead of bending over, I had difficulty remembering that only last February I had won bronze at the Olympics. The crouched, aerodynamic position of a speed skater made my body scream for relief after thirty seconds. It was a stretch to imagine that I would be ready for the World Cup races that began the first weekend of November.

When my team left Calgary for nine days of altitude training in the mountains of Utah, Coach Xiuli and physiologist Doc Smith decided to leave me behind. They thought it too taxing for me to train in the mountains after a summer of oxygen-laden cycling. My desire—call it my ego if you will—told me otherwise, but ego can get you into trouble.

Even during the first week of training, Xiuli had kept me away from the group, allowing me to do only a measly five laps in warm-up. Meanwhile, my teammates sailed around the ice in their sleek black training suits like otters in water. It seemed unfair, even though I knew they had been practising the skating posture for months in the off-season before slowly progressing onto the ice. As I awkwardly tried to balance on one foot while crouching with my leg out to the right, then to the left, my skating muscles, dormant after a summer of pedalling, let me know how much I needed these rudimentary exercises.

When team skating, I was fine until we came to the first corner, and my instincts failed to click in. While the long line of skaters shifted from straightaway strides to corner strides, I panicked: *What do I do? Oh, I turn . . . turn left!* It's amazing how something so practised can suddenly feel strange. After a split second that felt like an eternity, I shifted into those same corner strides. As the aches in my skating muscles subsided, I felt like a happy-go-lucky kid again. Surely gliding is the most glorious way for a human to move.

When my team returned, I was at last allowed to skate with them. As I joined the black train, chugging in perfect formation around the track, I realized that skating by myself had given me an opportunity to relearn, stride by stride, who I was as a skater, and why I had so joyfully returned to the ice. Another straightaway, then another corner, and I was striding along in unison. We were poetry in motion, each skater making up a line, each lap a verse, with the *swoosh* of the weight transfer and the click of our klap skates marking the rhythm.

During the 2002–3 season, our training was restructured with the goal of making us more of a team. Suddenly, I found myself actually getting to know the women I had travelled with for two years.

Xiuli had been promoted to national coach, and soon she had our little gang—Tara Risling, Kristina Groves, Cindy Klassen, Catherine Raney, and me—kicking ass all over Europe. Each woman was having the season of her life, and I was on the podium almost every competition. We broke the stranglehold of the German women on distance skating in World Cup events to become a force. Coaches, team leaders, skaters, therapists all began to ask: "What are you doing in Calgary? What's your secret?"

Our "secret" was hard work, Xiuli's coaching abilities, and the fact that each of us came to believe that the success of a teammate was a victory for us all. This unity was something we fed off. It was beautiful; it was fun; it was our weapon. We clued each other in on ice conditions. We stood by the track and shouted encouragement. We proved we were among the finest women skaters in the world.

By March 2003, Team Canada had one last big European trip on the horizon. Though my motivation was high, I was beginning to dream of returning home to Peter in beautiful Glen Sutton. It had been a long haul. It was time to sit in our backyard and listen to the birds. I missed Peter because he had spent that winter hiking the Long Trail in Vermont, while I had again rented a room from Tanya Dubnicoff in Calgary.

When everything is flowing smoothly, it's human nature to assume that life will continue the same way. We forget that fine line we tread moment by moment to exist, to stay healthy, especially when participating in any risky sport.

On this unlucky day, I was down in Tanya's basement, collecting my equipment for the next World Cup, in the Netherlands, to be followed by the World Single Distance Championships in Berlin. I'd already packed my eighteen-pound Trek racing bike, and now I was disassembling my touring bike, which I used all winter to get around. Carelessly, I lifted this steel-framed beast as if it was my light racer, and that's when it happened. My back seized. It was spasming so hard, I couldn't stand up. It was the most intense, vomit-inducing, inescapable pain I'd ever experienced.

I was alone in the basement, feeling like my spine had snapped, cursing myself for being so stupid. Slowly and painfully, I crept upstairs to the living room, where I lowered myself onto a couch. I attempted to get into skating position. Searing pain shot through my body.

I called Xiuli. She hurried over with a strange brown patch from China. "Put this on, it will help."

It didn't.

We contacted Lorrie Maffey, a physiotherapist who would be travelling with our team the next day, and a plan was formed.

After I'd checked in and cleared customs at the Calgary airport, Lorrie opened shop in the waiting area. With coats covering the dirty rug, I lay facedown so she could massage my tight back muscles, perform an ultrasound treatment, then crack my back so loudly that travellers not already staring turned to look. The relief Lorrie provided made it possible for me to survive the flight.

•   •   •

Heerenveen, where long blades rule and hockey skates are unusual, was the one World Cup event that would be hosting all the distances that year, instead of separating the endurance teams and sprinters.

The different dynamics between the two types of racers became apparent from our first meal together. Just as the fast-twitch fibres in the sprinters' legs instantly fired, those athletes quickly and good-humouredly ridiculed one another, while we quieter endurance athletes, as in a race, often didn't register a good comeback until many hours later. It was fun to be around humans who fired on all cylinders all the time. After watching these Ferraris zoom around the track, we must have looked like go-karts, especially long-distance freaks like me, with essentially one speed that could be held for 5000 metres. The Germans had dubbed me "the bicycle girl."

It took four weeks for my back to heal, and, while I was no stranger to pain, nothing compares to the incessant screech of an injured back. By the World Single Distance Championships, I began to feel that I had peaked. During the 5000 metres, I concentrated on my magic word— *EKWA!*—and I won silver. I was still disappointed, because without my injury I could have won gold.

I had been away from Glen Sutton for seven and a half months, except for ten days over Christmas, which served more as a tease to my home-sickness than a solution. Nothing could fill my heart like the sound of silence in the mountains of Quebec. As I sat with Peter, sipping coffee and admiring the soft early-morning light draping our valley in shades of spring, I recognized this as the moment I had been dreaming about while on the road. And yet . . . the lure of distance, of travel, of movement soon took over, as Peter and I knew it would.

We flew to California, then started our Baja tour from Chula Vista. That mountainous peninsula, which has a paved road about 1700 kilometres in length, awaited us once again. It was also a great way for me to get into condition after a gruelling season of racing. Sad to say, fitness is actually lost while competing because it's necessary to cut back on training volume to peak at race time. That lost endurance must be built back, kilometre by kilometre, and bike touring is the finest way to do this. One moves slowly enough to load the senses with sound, sight, and smell, yet fast enough to cover great distances.

We planned to ride 90 kilometres a day on our mountain bikes, road-rigged with semi-slick tires. Making these distances by the power of our legs felt liberating. The jungle of cactus lining the man-made vein of concrete running the length of Baja, with its shortening and lengthening shadows, seemed mysterious. Camping in its tangle felt potent yet peaceful, while the anonymity gave me energy and freedom, both powerful fuels after my months on public display.

Though we intended to stick to paved roads, as usual the lure of the backcountry proved too strong. We ended up riding on washed-out dirt tracks. Eventually—perhaps inevitably—my back started hurting again, putting me in a terrible mood, which Peter was forced to endure.

After almost a month, we reached our destination at the southern tip of the peninsula, Cabo San Lucas. We decided to bus back to San Diego instead of flying, because we thought that would be fun. Wrong. It was plain boring to sit on the bus watching the landscape pass by at 90 kilometres an hour, and when I lifted my bike onto a San Diego tram, I blew out my back again. Same bike, now loaded with all my touring gear. Same careless move. Same injured back. I was thirty years old, and my body knew it. I no longer had my youthful strength and flexibility. Not fun.

Now, faced with the upcoming cycling season, I decided that I didn't want to race. When I confessed this to Eric, he said, "Clara, this is not the way for you to bow out of the sport you've lived for such a large part of your life. Take a few weeks off, and when you're ready, we'll prepare for the Pan Am Games."

I agreed.

I went to the 2003 Pan Ams in the Dominican Republic. I won gold in the points race. I won silver in individual time trial. I won bronze in individual pursuit. Without enjoying any of it. I stood on the podium, with medals around my neck, smiling for everyone to see, while thinking: *This isn't me anymore. I won those races because I'm gifted and because I trained, and not because I loved riding my bike.*

I told Eric: "Enough!"

And so, I returned to skating full-time.

On November 6, our team set off for Hamar, Norway, to begin the 2003–4 season. The start is always exciting, like being presented with a field of untrammelled snow on which to carve the unknown future.

Travelling as a team is complicated business. Most often we're seen in airports, train stations, and hotel lobbies, wearing the red and white of the Canadian flag, strengthening our sense of solidarity, but blocking the way of other passengers as we wait like sheep for our coaches to herd us. Some passersby called a friendly "O Canada!" while others gave in to travel rage.

From Norway, we would be travelling by train, by bus, by air to the Netherlands, to Germany, suffering from jet lag, unexpected delays, and the stale, recirculated air in closed vehicles. As we crept through the European landscape, littered with leftover autumn hues, the beauty of the rolling hills made me wish I was on my bike, before I reminded myself I was not a two-wheeled creature anymore.

Every season is different. Individuals who shone in the past may have dimmed, while others gained lustre. This year we weren't doing as well—we were strong but not sharp. As autumn waned, we fought our way back to the top, where we belonged, with the best skaters in the world.

I decided to celebrate my return to full-time skating with a new pair of skates. Where else to make such a momentous choice but in the Netherlands, where the klap skate had been invented, allowing Dutch skaters to smash world titles before they were adopted by other countries?

My $1400 skates, purchased on my return to the ice, had won me a bronze in the 2002 Olympics. They had taken me through two seasons, but now, inevitably, they were falling apart. During a World Cup in Holland, I visited the Viking factory, along the highway between

Amsterdam and Heerenveen. Plastered on the stark-white walls of the waiting room of the modern factory were posters of famous Viking skaters, decorated in Olympic gold, silver, and bronze. A TV in the corner played a documentary on a century of Dutch skating, putting some of those poster images into motion. Encased in glass were different models of skates Viking had produced over the years, showing the evolution of our sport.

I wanted the classic model, like my old skates, not the sleek new ones with the zip-up lace covers. After trying on numerous pairs, I found the perfect fit, as if custom-made. Once again I felt as excited as I had been at age sixteen, with the purchase of my second-hand blades for $800. And the price was right—they were a gift from Viking as a reward, I suppose, for remaining loyal to tradition in the age of moulded custom boots. After promising to send Viking a signed photo in thanks, I felt strange imagining my picture on the waiting room wall among the icons of the sport.

Finally, we arrived at our last destination of the season—the World Single Distance Championships in Seoul, Korea, the biggest race of the year. Judged by the results, this season had hardly been my best. Instead of becoming demoralized, though, I grew more motivated by the wise words of Lao Tzu that Peter had sent to me: "Those who want strength must preserve it with weakness."

Because my body was tired and my competitive fire somewhat dimmed, I turned to technique and perspective as tools I could hone. With the help of my coaches, I worked on feeling my technique, bringing me closer to transforming skating into a moving meditation.

Instead of panicking when I caught laryngitis, I accepted illness as if it were planned, a part of my preparation, while also working to heal my ailing throat and lungs. I felt so aware, so ready for anything, that if someone had thrown marbles on the ice, I could have skated on them, telling myself they belonged there. I saw the ice and my opponents as the unknown to be cautiously and wisely explored, and I was aware that both were capable of surprises that would require me to be flexible.

Our team flew from Calgary to Seoul on March 4 for a ten-day visit, carrying speed skating into one of the world's most densely populated cities. We wandered around in awe, amid the fast-paced flow of cars and people, the neon signs, and the mammoth flat-screen billboards flashing commercials high above the hustle. It's not often that I feel like a complete outsider, and as the races approached, I could see the stress of this foreign land also reflected in the faces of my colleagues. Not understanding the language was frustrating. All I could muster was a pathetic version of "thank you"—*gamsa hamnida*—most often met with a look of confusion. Even at the speed-skating venue, I was virtually anonymous—a long-track speed skater in a land where short track rules.

The ice was in such poor condition that I told myself I was hockey skating, as if this were good news. The day before the 3000-metre race, I even welcomed the feeling of "heavy legs," as if reacquainting myself with an old friend. It was yet another reminder that I would have to work with what the day offered, be it a lightness of being or the heaviness of reality.

Since Xiuli—a new mother—was back in Calgary, I met with the other coaches on-site, accepting their guidance and precious words of encouragement. While on the massage table, receiving my daily treatment from Ed Louie, I would run through my newest insights, which included purging my thoughts of success based on results.

The morning of the 5000 metres, I received a call from Peter in California: "I'm really happy for you, Clara." Again, nothing about winning, just acknowledgement of how hard I'd struggled through so many years to find peace in the here and now.

At the oval, I walked through its icy tunnel, singing a song that I'd heard the night before. As I climbed the steps, I heard that song being pumped out trackside—synchronicity! My agility exercises, completing my warm-up, felt snappy and sharp, and as I skated I felt the ideal tempo I'd established in the previous day's 3000 metres take over. I wanted to accept the inevitable pain of exertion as a reward for my efforts, not as a punishment. I wanted to be motivated but not too motivated . . . everything in balance.

The pistol fired.

Something outside of me took over. I was inside my moving meditation. Stride after stride, I was close to matching the speed of my 3000-

metre race. *Should I be afraid of this?* I told myself: *Don't judge.* I wanted to discover what was possible without holding back.

With five laps to go, the effort felt close to killing me. I adapted my technique not only to skating but also to dealing with fatigue. I ignored the muscles that screamed for me to stop the abuse. With three laps to go, I was in such a drunken state of oblivion, caused by the buildup of lactic acid, that I was sure only one lap remained. The pain was so deep, I thought: *It has to be only one.* I waited to hear the bell that signalled that final lap. Silence. *Had someone forgotten to ring it?* Nope. I still had 800 metres left.

One lap later, I finally heard that bell, telling me: *Fight, and you have a chance.* It wasn't in me to bow to pain, so I found my second wind: *Push, push, push . . .*

Those were two of the longest laps in my life, yet I managed to hold my pace to the finish. Then, all I could do was snowplough to a stop and collapse on the nearest bench. My legs would no longer support me, and I thought I was going to explode from the agony of the effort. When the timekeepers congratulated me it seemed less significant than my personal satisfaction at having transcended pain to meet the challenge. I felt elated as I slowly began to move around.

After cheering for my teammates in the following pair, I went down to the changing room. I couldn't bear to watch the remaining skaters—not so much over concern for my final placement but because I didn't want to allow my satisfaction to be altered by what others were doing. I knew I had executed as close to a perfect race as possible at that time in my life. I had reached my capacity.

Eventually I did return to the oval, and the final pair had two laps to go, with their suffering visible on their faces. I wondered what they were thinking but was relieved it was over for me.

When I saw the final result, with my name at the top—World Championship gold—I didn't know how to react. I'd already experienced elation at achieving the race of my dreams, but it was rewarding to share these feelings with my coaches and my teammates.

I so wished Peter was present in more than just spirit. And Xiuli.

After our celebratory banquet, Ed Louie helped me sum up my

feelings: "Ice is just a bunch of frozen water. Like water in a stream, sometimes it's fast, sometimes slow. You have to work with the flow to make the most of it, whereas if you fight the current, all you do is waste energy. Fast water, like the fast ice in Calgary, carries you along, while slow water, like the ice in Seoul, requires more effort."

I had found the best way to work with the elements, not against them—just a bunch of left-hand turns on frozen water, so simple when looked at dispassionately, yet so complicated when overloaded with emotion, pressure, and expectation. I had accepted those twelve and a half laps and let them flow through me, so that for 7 minutes and 10.66 seconds, I had been one with the elements.

Once back again in the solitude of Glen Sutton, with the physical pain of Seoul erased, I could sit with a gold box holding a gold medal and wonder: *Can this really be true?* And then: *What does it mean to be a World Champion?* I knew how lucky I was—not to have this material reward but to have had the experience that resulted in this golden souvenir. To reach peak performance was to experience the rapture of being alive, not fixating on a specific outcome but feeling the wonder of the moment. Focusing on a goal makes you dependent on the actions of others and the vagaries of chance. On any given day, I could never say, "I am going to be the fastest." I must instead go into each experience with the idea of finding out what the fleeting moments offer.

Such was that special time for me in Seoul.

17

TORINO OLYMPICS 2006

Just when you think you have it all, it starts to slip away . . .

The 2004–5 skating season had been my best yet, taking me to my second Winter Olympics, in Torino, but I started partying hard again. I was alone on the road, and it just happened. With high-level athletes—perhaps with high-level anything—you often assume an all-or-nothing attitude that spawns what-the-hell behaviour. Especially when you're drinking and smoking and staying up half the night, yet still posting good results. You think you can do anything, because for a while you can.

I went to bed loaded too many nights. At the 2005 World All-Round Championships in Moscow, I won bronze in the 5000 metres, then became so drunk I almost missed the airport bus the next morning at six. Xiuli found me fumbling around the hall, aghast to see an athlete of hers so hammered. I didn't have a key; I couldn't get into my room and hadn't packed. She got me in, then rounded up all my stuff. When I stumbled into the shuttle, where the rest of the team was waiting, I was confronted by a lot of pissed off looks.

Peter, who had no idea I was leading such a self-destructive life, visited me at the World Single Distance Championships in Inzell, Germany. I won silver in the team pursuit and bronze in the 5000 metres, then shocked my moderate husband by the number of drinks I tossed back at the bar.

He asked, "What are you doing? This is stupid." He left me still drinking with the Russians.

I don't know how I made it back to our room—I suppose someone helped me. I was sick, threw up in the shower, then fell asleep on the bathroom floor.

Peter left for Canada the next morning, having made clear how disappointed he was in me. I had convinced myself that I was having a great time on the circuit, but when someone I loved saw me as a loser despite my external success, I was forced to take a hard look at myself. Xiuli was also fed up with me. She insisted that I promise not to get drunk until after the Torino Olympics, then made me shake hands on that. It was a promise I would keep.

Though I was glad to blame the pressures of racing, I was learning once again that I couldn't outskate or outcycle the gnawing darkness I carried inside myself, no matter how many shiny medals I won. My addiction, and whatever powerful emotions it covered up, was still something I was unwilling to confront. Sometimes I turned to alcohol, sometimes to food. When I had a day off from training, I could hear Mirek's voice in my head, berating me for being lazy, depressing me even more. Then I would overeat, turning myself into a guilty failure.

In the spring of 2005, I returned to Glen Sutton. Rather than work out with the team during April, I wanted to keep in condition by cycling with Peter. Xiuli agreed, though coaches usually stick with their athletes during the off-season, especially so close to an Olympic Games. Because I had been training and racing for so many years, Xiuli knew I needed a longer leash. She also recognized that as the only married athlete on her team, I needed time alone with my husband, sharing something we loved. She trusted me to undertake an intense adventure with Peter that would make me fit and strong.

After pulling out an atlas, I suggested, "Why don't I just open it up, and whatever page we see, that's where we'll go?"

That's how we ended up in southwest Arizona, riding on dirt and paved roads near the Mexican border, then up the east side of the state into the Navajo Nation. What a phenomenal trip, thanks to both the Navajo culture and the ever-changing landscape! Unfortunately, I became violently ill while camping at the Navajo National Monument, dry-heaving for fourteen hours straight. I felt like I'd been poisoned—a possibility we traced back to untested spring water. As I lay flat in our tent with my legs sticking out, a Navajo man stopped to ask, "Is she dead?" That's how bad I looked—yet another of the unconventional, not recommended ways I found of getting myself to racing weight.

When I was strong enough, some kind national park wardens drove us a hundred miles out of their way, because they said the area wasn't safe for hitchhiking. We slept overnight at a gas station campground, then hitched, holding a little cardboard sign saying: FLAGSTAFF. A Navajo couple drove us all the way to Phoenix. The driver was a Vietnam vet who took us through Sedona so we could see the desert shimmering like gold in the heat of the day.

After Arizona, I returned to Olympic boot camp. Having won gold, silver, and multiple team pursuits at World Cup events, I had already pre-qualified for the Torino Games. By now I really felt like a speed skater, instead of a cyclist who pretended to skate—that is, until I came down with pneumonia seven weeks before the Games. I was so sick that if I hadn't pre-qualified, I wouldn't have made the Olympics.

Though it had taken several years, I now trusted Dr. Smith, our physiologist. Despite his reliance on numbers and graphs, he also understood the human spirit. After Xiuli and I had trained together for six years, we were getting on each other's nerves. I felt she wasn't giving me the attention I needed to improve my technique now that she was so busy as national coach, and she disliked some of my behaviour. It just seemed natural to annoy each other after working so closely for so long. Doc Smith, who oversaw all the national teams, and Scott Maw, who functioned as his eyes on the ground, were crucial in mediating between Xiuli and me.

After I caught pneumonia, my body composition tests indicated that sometimes I would gain ten pounds in two weeks, and sometimes I would lose weight. I was so bummed out and depressed by the illness and the antibiotics that I overate to make myself feel better. I can remember munching junk food while watching multiple episodes of the TV show *Alias,* not what an elite athlete should be doing, but my way of making it through the day. Doc Smith didn't lecture me, but he told me the truth. The day before I left for Torino, my body composition was 23 percent fat, the worst I'd ever been, because I'd been unable to train for two weeks while being careless about nutrition.

As I looked at my pudgy self in the mirror, I remembered the male cyclists at last year's Tour de France, fighting it out, day after day, appearing emaciated even with their suntans and shockingly bright Lycra skin suits. That malnourished look meant they were *en forme* to fly up the mountains. As I confronted my reflection, I thought: *Wow, this sucks! But it is what it is.* That included my dark-ringed panda eyes.

Torino, Italy, February 10–26

Eighty nations were represented by 2508 athletes competing in 84 events. *So let the Games begin!*

Yeah, right. Except I felt weak and uninspired. I would have liked to go to the Opening Ceremony. Instead, I watched on TV, because my first race fell on the second day, and I felt like crap.

It wasn't just my health and lack of drive that bothered me. On our arrival in Italy, the Athletes' Village was only half done, and the oval was unimpressive. More important, the wonderful *Go, team, go!* spirit that had enflamed our Canadian women's team during our 2002–3 season had dissipated. Before these Games, we'd attended a week-long team-building camp, where we suffered through a nonstop schedule of workshops, motivational speakers, whitewater rafting, canoeing, go-karting, skits about the Olympics, and an Olympic version of *The Amazing Race*. It was supposed to build unity, but because speed skating is such an individual sport, it didn't work. Those who pretended to be great team players ended up being the most selfish when we returned to the reality of racing. While I was sick, nobody called to see how I was. When I came back, none of my teammates acknowledged me—not one single consoling or concerned word. That hurt.

After I confided in Xiuli and Peter, both told me the same thing: "Just harden up. Don't try to be helpful to the others, because you're not going to get anything back."

I took their advice, despite some serious annoyances.

After a pre-Torino training race during which I was still fighting pneumonia, one coach openly questioned whether I was good enough for the team pursuit. In his words: "We have to make sure Clara doesn't get left behind." *Oh, yeah, sure. How considerate.* In fact, we won silver at Torino in the team pursuit. *So, no. Clara didn't get left behind.*

That same coach made sure our team pursuit practices were organized around his skater's interviews, then arranged for the team's substitute athlete to skate with her. When I took the lead in telling him only team members should skate with us, the sub was stopped from tagging along, but the bad vibes persisted and our morale was low.

Before the 3000 metres I was skating poorly, as well as fighting with Xiuli. My skate technician, Alex Moritz, took me to watch the Chinese team practise short track, pointing out how they took their corners, using pressure to connect every inch of their blades to the ice, transferring their strength to speed. I tried to wrap my mind around the idea of relaxed power and effortless control while allowing myself to be propelled forward but ended up skating too hard in my warm-up. I was in the last pair. The winning time was not fast, and I thought I would win for sure. I started slowly, and no matter what I did, I couldn't go faster or even slower; I was like a robot circling around a set track. Every lap time was the same, and I ended up way down in ninth.

I wasn't the only one who was unhappy. Before the 3000-metre race, Xiuli couldn't be found, because of all the conflict with the other Canadian coach. Afterward, I saw that she'd been crying.

For the first week of the Games, I wandered around in a vortex of negativity, watching my teammates win medal after medal while I had only our team pursuit silver tucked away in my drawer. I spoke to a skier from Alpine Canada, who complained about his coaches having sealed him inside the Olympic dome. They had ordered him not to watch or explore or experience anything in order to *focus, focus, focus.* "I've been to two Olympics, and they've been the worst experiences of my life."

The advice the skier received had the opposite effect on me. A few days before the 5000 metres, I decided to take in more of the Olympic experience—anything to distract me from how bad I felt on the ice.

This decision led me to the booth of Right to Play, a Toronto-based organization founded by former Norwegian speed skater Johann Olav Koss, winner of four Olympic gold medals. Since retiring from competition, Johann had trained as a physician, then combined his medical and athletic expertise to use sport to help youth in disadvantaged countries. I was deeply moved by what I saw.

That feeling continued into the evening, when I watched American Joey Cheek, who'd just won the men's 500 metres, announce on TV that he was donating his winnings to Right to Play to help the children of Darfur. That seed money—$25,000—would eventually attract $500,000 when others matched it.

Both Kristina Groves, who was watching with me, and I wondered if we had it in us to do the same thing. Neither of us was sure. As Canadian athletes, our situation was different from that of the Americans and skaters from many other nations, since we would not be receiving reward money for winning in Torino. However, I knew that I did have $10,000 in the bank. I asked myself: *If I win a medal, could I use the podium to turn my $10,000 into a much larger donation, as Joey had?*

With this thought as a spur, I decided to change my Olympian experience by shifting my attitude from *I can't skate* into *Maybe this is how I'm supposed to feel before winning the Olympics.* That had worked for me in Seoul, when I won gold in the 5000 metres, so why not now? I took the little sparkle I found hidden inside myself and built on it, so that it twinkled a bit more each day.

The night before the 5000-metre race, Xiuli came to my room with the pairings. She asked: "Do you really want to know?"

I exclaimed, "Oh, no, not Claudia Pechstein!"

She nodded. "Yes, you're with Claudia. The outer lane."

For me, it was the worst pairing possible, because every time I skated with Claudia, she got the better of me. She'd make lane changes that were problematic for me, or accelerate so that I'd have to slow down, or speed up coming out of the corner. The first time I was paired with her, in Heerenveen, I finished second while she won the World Cup. Her coach—an old, slick East German—stood in the middle of the lane, where I was supposed to skate, holding Claudia's lap board. I was sure I was going to hit him till he jumped away at the last minute, having first messed up my rhythm.

After the race I told him, "Hey, asshole, don't ever do that to me again!" Then I told Claudia, "Remind your coach to get out of my way. Do you think I'm stupid?" She pleaded ignorance, and I cried no tears a few years after Torino when Claudia was suspended for suspected blood doping, causing her to miss the Vancouver Games.

During our confrontation, one of my coaches, Gregor Jelonek, took me aside, saying, "Clara, relax, you're on television. Don't you realize you've given the Germans what they want? From now on, they're going to hassle you every time because they know how to get to you." Because I was still livid, it took me a while to understand that Gregor was right.

Starting in the outer lane wasn't good either. When you start in the outer, you finish in the outer. You don't get that last slingshot into the inner lane that might win the race. When I complained about this to Xiuli, she was so tired of me she said: "Clara, there's nothing you can do. Why don't you talk about what you *can* accomplish instead of what you can't?"

While Xiuli and I were arguing, I was sure Claudia and her coach were figuring out how to work me over during the race. They were glad Claudia was paired with me.

I told Xiuli: "Okay, if she goes fast, I'll go slow. If she slows down, I'll go fast. I'm going to do the opposite of what she wants. And if her coach stands in my way, I'll run him over."

After developing this strategy, I decided that my pairing with Claudia might be the best possible, because I knew what I'd be dealing with. There were no unknowns.

After Xiuli left, I felt empty and alone, with only my worried thoughts. To distract myself, I turned on the TV. A Swiss silver-medal winner was figure-skating to an awful James Blunt song but creating some of the most beautiful figures I'd ever seen. He was dressed in black and moving with total freedom and joy, spinning and gliding and jumping and swaying. I was so impressed that I wrote *Joy* on my hand, reminding myself that's how I wanted to skate the following day. After that, I went to sleep with a smile on my face.

•   •   •

On the morning of the 5000 metres, I had coffee and breakfast, then did a little spin on my rollers. I found myself in that familiar place of passing time: not thinking too much, not thinking too little; not resting too much, or too little; not talking too much, just having light conversations. I had a long day to put in because I did not race until six that evening.

When I turned on the TV set, CBC was showing a Right to Play documentary about Uganda, featuring Canadian Olympians—Steve Podborski, a downhill skier, and Charmaine Crooks, a sprinter. I watched, mesmerized, as former child soldiers, born into war and poverty and HIV/AIDS, engaged in play as if they had no worries. They were dirt poor and so shy as they sneaked glances at the cameras, then quickly turned away.

I looked at the word on my hand, and then the faces of the children, and I told myself: *You're going to win the Olympics, and you're going to give your own $10,000 to Right to Play.*

Joy became my mantra.

I moved through the rest of that day as if through a dream. I envisioned the race unfolding—me being behind at the beginning, then coming on strong in the final two laps. All I had to do was bring myself to the line, then not waver from my mission, which was far greater than simply winning.

When I showed up at the oval, the first person I saw was Claudia. She was cordial, saying, "Hey, how's it going?" I thought: *You think you're going to work me over, but you have no idea how on to you I am.*

We were the last pair to race. I went through my warm-up on the ice, which was simply a reminder that I knew how to skate. I made no special effort and felt neither good nor bad.

I remember standing on the line, hearing myself introduced to the packed venue by name, country, and past successes. Because Claudia was the three-time defending champion, her ovation was enormous. Even though I'd won the World Cup and was World Champion two years before, my accomplishments paled beside Claudia's. I wanted to destroy her. The English announcer was Matt Jordan, my strength trainer who worked the big competitions, which I took as a good sign. I stood fiddling with my glasses, thinking: *Just shoot the gun.*

Glancing up into the crowd, I noticed a little girl in braids holding a paper Canadian flag and a sign with big red letters: FORZA CLARA. It was Rebecca, from the family whose house we were renting for Peter. Her eyes had that look of hope and jubilation that I'd seen in those kids from Uganda, thanks to Right to Play. I told myself: *Don't look up again because you'll lose it.* I glanced at my hand instead—*Joy.*

The gun fired.

Almost immediately, it seemed Claudia and her coach started playing their tricks. I was a little behind Claudia, but both of us were behind Cindy Klassen's posted time by seven seconds. I had told Xiuli, "I don't want to know where I am compared to the fastest time because I'm going so fast at the end I'll make up any deficit."

I felt relaxed, then I tightened up, and Xiuli yelled at me to relax again and to breathe. The crowd was quiet. The Dutch had skated terrible races, and because we were so far behind Cindy's time, the spectators thought this was a dud event. At first, there was no enthusiasm whatsoever as Matt counted down the laps, but we were inching closer to Cindy's winning time, and the crowd realized they were potentially witnessing the gold-medal race. By the time I started to feel the pain, they were shouting.

With about three laps to go, I caught sight of Claudia in my peripheral vision, and she was looking a little tired, not as awesome as usual. I knew she was cracking, and that's when I had to attack. At precisely the point when knives pierced every muscle, I let the roar of the crowd ring in my ears, as if someone had switched off the mute button. I channelled the energy, drank it in, while repeating *Lower, longer, stronger,* and suddenly, I was going faster. With one more lap on the inner, I was even with Claudia. I urged myself to go as hard as possible because Claudia would have my draft on the last lap, which would slingshot her into the inner for a win. I skated like someone was chasing me with a knife. As I went down the backstretch, I could see Claudia's coach, but I didn't care. I was going to run him over if he got in my way. By my last outer, I was in agonizing pain. I couldn't see Claudia in my peripheral vision, so I focused on the finish line: *Just get me there.*

I threw my blade across that line, knowing I'd beaten Claudia, the three-time 5000-metre Olympic winner. Only then did I look at the numbers. I had broken the seven-minute barrier—*6:59.07!* I screamed, putting my head in my hands. I'd just won gold at the Olympics!

My body gave out and I collapsed, lying on the ice, sick with pain. When I turned my face, I saw Xiuli. She whispered, "I know you're hurting, but people are watching. You are on television. You should stand up."

After some coaxing, I managed not only to stand but to skate a lap with the Canadian flag flying high over my head, like an enormous wing, allowing me to feel it—pure joy. I, too, was flying.

As I stood on the podium, with my teammate Cindy Klassen, who'd won bronze, I heard them play "O Canada." I found my voice, and I knew it was time to use it. I brought Cindy onto the top step of the podium with me so we could sing together. She had won her fifth medal of the Games, and I had done the impossible in winning the 5000 metres.

Afterward, I went to a press conference, where I announced that I was going to donate $10,000 to Right to Play, then challenged Canadians to donate more. CBC host Brian Williams invited me onto his show, and by the end of the next day, $100,000 had been raised. Four months later, it had grown into $430,000.

I met up with Peter, and we went to a bar across the street from the oval. He said, "You know, I can't believe you pulled that off. No one was talking about you. Everyone thought Claudia was a cinch to win. Or Cindy. I didn't enjoy watching at all, and afterward, I thought you were having a heart attack."

The two of us laughed, and we probably didn't stop laughing for the whole night.

I had won a race that physiologically I should not have been able to win.

Doc Smith agreed. When I returned to Calgary, he said: "You have proven everything I believe in to be wrong. You have a focus that I've never seen before that allows you to do anything, no matter what."

Such an acknowledgement, coming from him, was so cool.

18

RIGHT TO PLAY, RIGHT TO LIVE

The lesson I learned in Torino was this: For medals to mean something to me, they must stand for more than my having crossed the finish line faster than anyone else. Otherwise they were just souvenirs I sent to my mom in Winnipeg to share with family and friends. What earned me gold in Torino was not just my thousands of hours of training but my feelings of fierce commitment to Right to Play at a time when I was in no condition to medal. My professional life had intersected with my personal life, teaching me how to live.

Right to Play was the inspiration of one person—Johann Olav Koss. A few months before the 1994 Lillehammer Winter Olympics, Johann had travelled to Eritrea, in the Horn of Africa, on behalf of the organization Olympic Aid. While watching children play amid burned-out tanks that were the harsh legacy of decades of war, Johann noticed one boy who seemed especially popular. When he asked that boy for his secret, the kid replied, "I have long sleeves." Taking off his shirt, he rolled it up, using the sleeves to tie it into a ball that all the children could toss around. Johann was astonished. Here were kids, in the aftermath of violence, still eager to play.

At the Lillehammer Olympics, Johann made history by breaking three speed-skating world records and winning three gold medals. He pledged his gold-medal bonus to Olympic Aid, then asked Norwegians to donate a few dollars for every medal won by their national team. Norway won twenty-six medals, and Johann raised more than $18 million. When he flew to poverty-stricken Eritrea with an airplane of sports equipment, the Norwegian media had one word for him: fool!

Johann apologized to Eritrea's president. "You needed food and I brought sports equipment."

The president was delighted. "For the first time, we are being treated like human beings, not just something to be kept alive."

In 2003, Johann reinvented Olympic Aid as Right to Play, guided by the principles of inclusion, child protection, and gender equality. Today, this organization, with its head office in Toronto, uses sport and play to help one million disadvantaged children in twenty countries to overcome poverty, conflict, illiteracy, and disease. Key to RTP's success is its skill in training local coaches to engage communities on the grassroots level while also winning the approval of each country's political leadership.

Why play? It's instinctive. RTP's motto: "Look After Yourself, Look After One Another."

Three months after the 2006 Torino Games, I was invited to serve as one of RTP's athlete ambassadors, which meant using my personal story and my experience in sports to inspire RTP leaders and kids in the field, then to raise awareness and funds for RTP programs back in Canada.

I was thrilled.

I have now travelled for RTP to Ethiopia, Ghana, Rwanda, Liberia, Uganda, Mali, and the West Bank, partly funded by CIDA (Canadian International Development Agency). I serve as a volunteer on RTP's International Board of Directors and also work with RTP staff to improve the athlete ambassador program.

My first trip took me, along with six others, to Ethiopia, located midway down the east coast of Africa. As our bus navigated through the bustling capital of Addis Ababa, with its combination of ancient monuments and contemporary high-rises, the impact of seeing such rampant poverty was like being hit by a truck: old women bent low under heavy loads; children in rags; beggars with disabilities crawling on the street; babies squatting in the dirt while parents sold their meagre goods. It was the sheer volume of neediness in this city of more than 3 million that got to me, yet so many people were smiling, even laughing and dancing.

My whirlwind trip left me filled with images, both inspiring and heartbreaking, that were hard to assimilate. RTP was active in schools for the blind, for the disabled, and for the mentally handicapped. They recruited as coaches kids who had lost arms or legs from land mines, breaking the stigma that had their parents keeping them at home. Because of increasing confidence, children in RTP programs did markedly better in school.

Though girls in Ethiopia were culturally excluded from sports beyond selected running programs, RTP had them playing in soccer leagues and tournaments. In these safe and respectful environments, spectators could see that the girls were really skilled. Some games had mothers good-naturedly playing against daughters, with the whole community turning out to see the fun. These scenes were powerful and moving for me.

I remember the professionalism of one teenaged RTP coach, who used symbolism attached to the Olympic rings to teach self-awareness. Red represented the mind; yellow, the spirit; green, health; blue, peace; black, physical fitness. Holding up the red ball, she explained to the children, "We have a special gift of our mind. Even in sports, you have to think about how you are going to win a game, so playing helps our thinking and our creativity."

Ethiopia was a steep learning curve for me, but what shone brightest was the ability of RTP leaders to pass down courage and optimism to the children. They were not thinking about what they didn't have or couldn't do. They were making their lives work, enriched by the wonderful opportunities RTP offered. As someone who, in the grind of training, often views athletics as a torture, I was gratified to see clear evidence of how sport and play can create a healthier and safer world.

While I was not yet experienced enough to evaluate my own participation, I did make one very clear connection. Ethiopia is known as a running mecca, with its middle- and long-distance competitors having set many world records. In Addis Ababa, I began early-morning runs, along with the hundreds of locals who filled the streets. Though I felt like an ox among these lithe, fleet-footed Ethiopians, they accepted me with waves and smiles, making the experience personal.

In 2007, I was inducted into the Order of Canada as a member, and in 2010 the honour was upgraded when I was inducted as an officer in recognition of both my athletic accomplishments and my work with Right to Play. I didn't take this as an award for anything I'd done but as a sign that I was on the right track. What's the point of celebrity, if not to be a platform to help others?

I travelled with Right to Play again in the spring of 2008, with three other Olympians, this time to Ghana, where more than thirty thousand kids were enrolled in RTP programs run by about seven hundred coaches.

Ghana, on the Atlantic coast, was the first African nation to declare independence from European colonization, in this case from Britain. We landed in Accra, the crowded, sprawling capital, which seemed to have as many goats as people. The next day, our group travelled along bumpy, dusty side roads to a primary school in Madina with an enrolment of four thousand. When our van pulled in, children smiled and waved. Later, as I participated in games, I could see kids pointing at me and giggling. Eventually, my Ghanaian partner of the moment grew bold enough to explain: "Your hair is bouncy."

"Pardon?"

"Your hair is BOUN-CY!"

Though I was used to children staring at my bright red hair, this was new.

When he jumped around to demonstrate, all the girls near me repeated, "Yes, bouncy!" Then they lined up to touch my hair.

Both here and at our next school, we winter athletes tried to explain our sports, which began with explaining snow and ice. The kids were polite and patient—they knew we had come a long way to see them, and that's what impressed them.

Our second school had only a few hundred students and no roof—it had blown away the year before, so when it rained, the kids were sent home. Given the lushness of the countryside, that probably happened a lot. Like the other students, these kids came from extreme poverty. I felt a mixture of sadness and joy when I saw how much RTP meant to them. Those feelings grew more profound in Battor, where we visited the Three Kings School for the mentally handicapped, who were so often neglected and abused. Though the facility was sombre, with open-air classrooms and no lights, the kids returned to us, over and over, to shake our hands, laughing all the while, before demonstrating RTP games for us.

In Tamale, Ghana's second-largest city, mud huts with grass roofs dominated the landscape. Here, in the Muslim north, life was notably tougher than in the Christian south. I was shocked to see so many men lounging in the shade while the women laboured under heavy loads and washed clothes in rivers choked with garbage. Some of the men had three or four wives, resulting in over a dozen children, often neglected. It is children like these whom RTP tries to protect by providing educational opportunities.

In neighbouring towns, the poverty was even more oppressive. Kakra Ankobiah, one of Tamale's program directors, told me about a boy he had met while working with an HIV/AIDS organization. The little guy was so brave, even while dying of AIDS. One day he asked six-foot-tall, built-like-a-linebacker Kakra, "Will I ever grow up to be as big and strong as you?" Kakra told the little boy, "You are already bigger and stronger than I will ever be, my friend." Like many others, Kakra had started working with RTP to help prevent HIV/AIDS through education.

At Bolgatanga, in dry, dusty northeast Ghana, the children played the RTP game Mosquito Clap. This involved killing mosquitoes while also stressing the value of mosquito netting. In a place where so many people die from malaria, it's surprising to think this was something that needed to be taught, but RTP leaders know their communities well.

Among the twenty-five thousand refugees in a camp near the shantytown of Buduburam were some who'd been displaced eighteen years previously by the Liberian civil war. When I talked with the kids, who wore a tough veneer, I tried to build hope but ended up feeling discouraged. Later, an RTP staffer told me he had asked a little girl how she felt about my visit, and she said, "It made me happy. One day I want to see Clara, the lady who played with me, on TV, so I can say, 'That's my friend.'"

After my week in Ghana, I met up with Peter in London, and we flew to Tel Aviv. We would be staying with Stephanie Jenzer, head producer for CBC in Jerusalem, who had covered RTP with us in Ethiopia. Though this was a personal trip for Peter and me, I had asked RTP to let us spend a day with their workers in the West Bank.

Our first stop was Ramallah, the administrative centre of Palestine. In a school for the blind, we met an RTP volunteer teacher, so strong and stern yet caring that she had made the RTP programs specific for her vision-impaired students. This encouraged them to feel that while they might be different, they were not disabled. It was wonderful watching them play so naturally.

We also visited two West Bank refugee camps. Since they dated from just after World War II, they had become crowded concrete cities. The families were multiple-generation refugees, and the kids had a wild feel about them. RTP programs were geared toward releasing that pent-up, aggressive energy in a positive way. By the end of the day, Peter and I must have played soccer and basketball with about three hundred Palestinian kids, sometimes with no nets and with one ball that deflated if it was stepped on. When we returned to Jerusalem, we learned from the evening news that conflict in Gaza had resulted in the death of five refugee-camp children, just like those we'd played with that afternoon. It made me realize the fine line these kids—just like the kids we met in the West Bank—were walking between life and death.

Even in Canada, the mention of Rwanda in central Africa stirs chilling images of the 1994 genocide between the Tutsis and the Hutus, resulting in possibly a million deaths, with an additional 2 million Hutus fleeing to neighbouring countries.

In the summer of 2010, I travelled with Right to Play to Rwanda. Despite a period of reconciliation, the country's wounds still ran deep. Before going out into the field, I was given "sensitivity training," in which I was told not to ask anyone in Rwanda about family, or their home city, or region, since this could stir up painful memories of lost loved ones.

On my first morning, I went for a run at 6:00. Everyone had assured me it would be safe, though I was nervous. It was Sunday, and local runners were everywhere—young and old, male and female, athletic and not so much. I simply went with the flow, travelling counterclockwise in a 1-kilometre loop. A teenager whom I'd been chasing stopped to do some standing tuck and pike jumps, demonstrating incredible vertical and explosive power.

I passed him as he was on tuck jump number fifteen or so.

Shortly after, I heard *thump-thump-thump* behind me, and soon I had a running friend. Then another. As the pace increased, I saw that I was being checked out to see if I was hurting. I put on my best poker face, then smiled. *"Ça va bien?"* The boy nodded and smiled, then on we went, lap after lap. The second kid took a rest lap while I and my remaining companion hammered out a good tempo. Each person or group we passed clapped and cheered, *"Courage!" "Bon courage a vous!"* I was the *Umuzungu,* meaning "whitey," with my sickly skin and orange hair. Even as a professional athlete, I felt inferior alongside kids with no shoes, displaying a running gait better than that of most of my speed-skating team, me included.

After an hour, covered in sweat, with my eyes burning and lungs scorched from the smoke and pollution, I was ready for a shower and breakfast. My running mate and I high-fived, after yet another example of sport breaking down barriers, and not at all what I had expected in Rwanda.

My tour of the Genocide Memorial with Jean-Philippe Marcoux, RTP's deputy regional manager for West and Francophone Africa, was a mood changer. I felt numb as I listened to the audio commentary at one of the many mass graves, especially the last section, dedicated to children. It was marked by beautiful poster-sized photos, with written material sharing each child's likes, favourite foods, best friends, personality traits ("a sweet girl"), and, finally, how each was killed.

In Rwanda I also had a privileged opportunity to see how locals were trained by RTP staff using the group's manual, *Live Safe, Play Safe.* Like skating, it looked easy when done well, hiding the enormous amount of planning that took place behind the scenes, including the careful coaching and evaluation of each candidate. One director told me he had been a street kid, foraging for food in garbage dumps, until the RTP programs rescued him.

These training sessions also reinforced the importance of discussions after the games, when children talked about how it felt to win or to lose, allowing them to apply the experience to their daily lives.

When I first met Massamba Gningue, country manager for RTP in Rwanda, he refused to shake my hand. "No handshakes, just hugs," he told me. It was Massamba who challenged me to go deeper in the telling of my personal story. I was hesitant, wondering how I could connect with these war-traumatized children while talking about a winter sport that made little sense to them. Massamba made assurances. "All they need to know is that being good at what you do took years of training, working through frustrations, and never giving up."

I reminded myself that kids are kids all over the world, so I told them how sport saved me from a self-destructive life on the streets, while encouraging them to find something to which they could commit, and even feel passionate about.

One older kid asked, "Are you a superstar?" and "Do you have everything?"

I replied, "Because I'm healthy and active, I feel very rich indeed. I also feel I have everything I need to achieve anything that's meaningful to me."

With a group of preschoolers, I did stretch exercises in a fun game of In the Sea, on the Land, though I was more than twice their size. I learned a few words in Kinyarwanda (*sea* and *land*), and we laughed a lot. At the RTP evaluation session, I was told that a few of the kids are always sent to school without lunches, so they go to a different room while the others eat.

Some boys found an empty toilet-paper roll, which they used to play one-on-one soccer, reminding me of Johann's "long-sleeved shirt" guy, and how kids will always instinctively find a way to play.

In a 35-kilometre drive into the hills from Kigali, our SUV wound its way along narrow mountain roads, through eucalyptus and pine trees. Once again, women and the smallest children were carrying huge loads of fruit, sugar cane, and water, usually on their heads. Rows of women with hoes lined the fields, hacking away at the earth to grow tea and corn.

At a school where some of the students were HIV positive, we did a drill that had us picking imaginary mangoes from imaginary trees— stretching up high, to the left, to the right, then down to put each mango in an imaginary basket. After that, we split into two groups for handball. Well, more like a version of handball. The field was grass and rock-hard clay, with no marked boundaries, goals, or nets. Game on meant a frenzy of running, passing, jumping, and sprinting to get the ball to one's goalie. Each player used a bin, hand-manoeuvred to catch a shot. The kids made that work because they wanted it to work. We laughed, high-fived, and gave each other thumbs-up after goals.

Post-game, the participants shared how it felt to support each other, and how they could bring those emotions to everyday life. Once again, I was learning the importance of play in forming character, underscoring why RTP activities are an approved part of the country's physical education and health curriculum.

After that, I told my story to hundreds of shiny-eyed kids, sitting on a hillside, hoping each would have a fighting chance, not only to survive but to thrive in their difficult world. It meant a lot to me when they sang in French: "We are happy that you came, and wish you good-bye."

At my last stop in Rwanda, I participated in a Live Safe, Play Safe event run by a Canadian priest who'd been there for thirty-eight years. After RTP trainees discussed marginalization, especially the stigma of HIV and AIDS, they played a game of Wild Dog that taught lessons about exclusion and inclusion. A teenager who had been abandoned by his parents because of a disability played along with us, no longer an outcast. At the end of the game, his good-bye hugs were the warmest.

Before leaving, I showed RTP trainees a brief video of me speed-skating, then passed around one of my medals for them to touch and share. It was fun to watch them look from me to the skin-suited crea-ture gliding on the ice. Afterward, I did a goofy dry-skating demonstra-tion for them, with one of the trainees joining in.

My Rwanda story had a postscript. A year later, while I was in a

Calgary taxi en route to the airport with my usual overabundance of sporting gear, I discovered that my driver was from Rwanda. Because of my sensitivity training, I told him about my positive experiences in his country, rather than asking questions.

Pumped by the conversation, he replied, "Ah, that's nice. Did you see the gorillas in the mist? They are incredible creatures. Rwanda has a lot of nice things. Since the genocide, it has really changed and is very safe."

Without prompting, he continued, "The genocide was very difficult for my country. I lost two brothers, two sisters, and my father. They were slaughtered. I was lucky to escape with three siblings and my mother. And for what? You look at us in Rwanda, we are all the same. We are all Rwandans. Somewhere, the difference was made between the Hutus and the Tutsis. Me, I am Tutsi. Do I hate the Hutus? No."

I sat. I listened. His humanity and the forgiveness were startling. I wondered if I would be able to feel the same under similar circumstances, but I couldn't even imagine being in those circumstances.

My driver added, "There will always be Hutus and Tutsis. We will both live in Rwanda together, that is not going to change. So we cannot hate each other."

He told me his mother did not want to leave her home, her culture, even though two of her surviving children were in Canada. My driver was an electrical engineer, well educated, like so many new Canadians who drive taxis. Even the loss of his career did not seem to faze him. He was a good sport as he unloaded my gear—two bikes, a stationary trainer, personal luggage, and a rolling carry-on bag—smiling the whole time and leaving me with a warm heart. This lesson in a taxicab on a cold winter's day showed me the potential of human beings to transcend hatred, greed, and genocide. Even now, I marvel that someone could come to this kind of peace after losing so much.

In the fall of 2011, I was off again for RTP, this time to Mali, in northwestern Africa, a former French colony that gained its independence in 1960.

Day 1 in the capital of Bamako proved to be a personal challenge. After years of global travel, I somehow managed to avoid packing any necessities in my carry-on. Therefore, when only one of my two checked bags arrived, I found I had my coffee supplies, my kettle, my workout gear (bands, wobble board, etc.), but no clothes beyond the boots, jeans, T-shirt, and jean jacket in which I'd travelled. With temperatures in Mali spiking to 34°C, these were useless. I was grateful when Sarah, a Canadian RTP staffer, and Jackie, the photojournalist accompanying us, lent me clothes. Canadian Adam van Koeverden, a gold-medal kayaker, supplied my size 12 feet with some flip-flops that were on the small side.

All this fuss over what to wear became trivial after I was briefed on what RTP had accomplished here in a decade. There's nothing like a dose of Africa as a reality check for my own cushy existence.

When the RTP programs began, the head of Mali's ministry of education did not believe in the effectiveness of sport and play in educating and motivating young people. That's when RTP staff started inviting local educators into the field to witness the changes in the kids firsthand. Not only had classroom absentee rates fallen but the kids demonstrated greater respect for their teachers, transforming them from the enemy into adults with something positive to share. The teachers were also learning better communication skills.

A main RTP focus is female engagement. In Mali, a country where sport for girls is uncommon, they were playing basketball and volleyball on an RTP-funded slab of concrete in the centre of the city. It stood out like an oasis in this densely populated area.

Don't Trust Your Eyes was an RTP game of deception in which HIV/AIDS awareness was taught through trivia-style questions asked of students when they wrongly guessed the location of a hidden ball. The game, which also incorporated the subject of gender equality, proved surprisingly fun.

On our second day, we were introduced to the sights and sounds of children playing on the "miracle" field created by moving a mountain. Or, at least, getting it to shove over.

In Banconi, just outside the capital, is a flat, open, clay-packed space that floats like a mirage among surrounding rocks, with rickety goal-posts marking each end. It was created in 1996 out of the desires of children in the community to have a place to play. After they cleared the trash-filled stream, out came pickaxes and shovels to tackle the mountain itself. Bit by bit, they levelled the rocky terrain. Bit by bit, their dream came true. Bit by bit, they created a space for themselves and for generations to follow.

As I looked down from the schoolyard above, I imagined those kids, with shovels or bare hands, heaving dirt and gravel, moving a mountain, because it was something they could do for themselves.

As I've said many times, a calm sets over me whenever I leave a city for the countryside, and in Africa that was no different. One morning we left early by SUV for a trip into rural Mali. Infrastructure was surprisingly good, with decent pavement between Bamako and the district of Bouroungi. After that, we made do with a bumpy, sandy vein of cleared vegetation, having to halt many times to manoeuvre through eroded land. Finally, a group of adobe huts with thatched roofs came into view. A phalanx of laughing, clapping children chanted, "Right to Play! Right to Play!" When I exited the vehicle, a swarm of little hands reached out, while smiling faces encircled me. The kids were too small to understand who we were, but their excitement at having visitors was real. Our welcome at every village was just as enthusiastic. As more than one elder told us, "That you came to visit means you care."

To the kids, we were just *tubabu,* or white people. Adam's sport and mine meant nothing to them. There was no ice, no organized bike racing, no kayaking. One village chief, blind in one eye, threw off his shoes, then danced with the energy of a child. He had the moves, and soon we were all clapping, laughing, and cheering.

"Now that's how you warm up!" he said in French.

Right to Play provided a motorcycle for the local doctor to travel from village to village to vaccinate the children. Simultaneously, their mothers were taught to make a porridge of corn flour fortified with powdered milk, fresh lime juice, and sugar, cooked for twenty-five minutes in a massive pot over an open fire. This was far healthier than the region's typical porridge, made only of corn or millet flour and water.

Mali has one of the highest infant mortality rates in the world. All these items were available, but in their culture they weren't mixed together. I'm always impressed how RTP shape-shifts to meet the needs of each community, while maintaining its core philosophies.

Later, I was happy to spend time with students in the Youth Initiative, which I am funding. While they were being taught leadership skills, I learned many were unable to write or read. One young man said he'd never written a letter in his life—and what he meant was he'd never written a single letter of the alphabet. A literacy component was added to the program. And a soccer league.

Back in Bamako, I was once again surrounded by diesel fumes. And goats. Goats filled every open space in preparation for the Fête du Mouton on November 6. The locals called them "sheep," but they definitely looked like goats to me. This was the most important day of the year, when each family sacrificed a sheep/goat to give thanks to God. Or Allah, as 90 percent of Mali's population is Muslim. We wondered how this could be a celebration of these animals, since they were sacrificed and eaten. Not a great day for them, I'd say, but is it any different from our relationship with turkeys at Thanksgiving? We are so removed from what we eat that we go to a grocery store, pick the fattest bird from the freezer, then defrost and cook it. Imagine turkeys crowding every Canadian street at Thanksgiving, awaiting their fate. That's what it was like in Mali. The whole process was public, which wasn't great to watch or remember.

On our last day, we visited a youth detention centre. I thought RTP might find it difficult to work with toughened young men, but soon we were all holding hands, playing handball, clapping, and singing. These youths had made mistakes, but RTP was there each week to lighten their load, in hopes of helping them change their futures.

That evening, our last, we celebrated with the entire RTP crew in Bamako, aided by food, music, and dance. Dance! Ever step onto a dance floor in Africa, with live music and the singer chanting your name?

I'm a much better athlete than a dancer, but my Olympic pal Adam killed it. Even the band's professional dancers were impressed. He kept up with the frantic progression of beats as the pros made the moves harder and more complex, adding his own moves in a counterchallenge. Adam kept Canada in the game.

Once again, RTP provided me with many windows through which to watch a different world. Once again, I'd felt the impact of the passionate commitment of staff and volunteers. They believed they could change lives with play, and after each hand that I shook, after each smile I shared, after each dream I heard, I believed that, too.

RECYCLING
2010–2012

19

FULL CIRCLE

After Torino I wasn't sure if I wanted to race anymore. Those Games had been such a high—a triumph of mind over matter that led to Olympic gold. Weren't athletes supposed to quit at the top? Sure, Vancouver and the lure of competing on home turf awaited, but in 2010, I would be thirty-seven, and I just didn't know if I wanted to continue to train/race/train/race for another four years. In fact, I didn't even know if I wanted to finish out the 2006 season.

When I spoke to Xiuli, she said, "You don't have to do anything you don't want to do."

In the end, I did go to Europe and China and Japan, with good, bad, and indifferent results. I certainly didn't feel like a defending champion on my way to the Vancouver Olympic Games.

While I struggled with my technique, Xiuli asked Johann Olav Koss, my Right to Play hero, for advice. He told me, "You're working against yourself. You can fix that in the turn by pointing your shoulders to the right, as if you were skating sideways. Just look to the right, and your shoulders will follow."

When I did this, it felt weird, but Johann had nailed it, and this helped me qualify for Vancouver.

My last World Cup event of the 2006–7 season was in Germany. Before the race, I had a call from Peter: His dad had died on February 14. Everyone was taken by surprise. Elías was eighty. He had lived with diabetes for about thirty-five years but was remarkably healthy and active. Though insulin-dependent, he would garden and hunt and forget to eat. Many times his blood sugar would drop so low he'd have to be rushed to the hospital. Peter and I had had a scare the year before when Peter's brother, Michael, had called to say, "If you want to see Dad alive, come home now." That time, though Elías was very sick, he pulled through, giving us the false sense that he always would.

This time, he hadn't.

Peter was always so considerate about my career that he only reluctantly called my hotel in Erfurt. He hadn't been sure if he should break this disturbing news before my last qualifying race for the World Championships. Of course, he was right to do so, and I was crying when I told Xiuli, "I have to go home. I have to be with Peter."

She agreed. "Family is more important. Let's change your ticket. We'll make it happen."

Within twelve hours I had boarded what was a packed plane to Calgary. Though this would be a ten-hour flight, I was already counting the minutes till I would be with Peter and his family—*my* family—so we could move through our sorrow together.

A second flight took me to the small airport in Eugene, Oregon. Green fields basked in gentle sunlight, in contrast to the snow-covered streets and fields of Alberta.

As soon as I saw Peter at the airport, I knew that leaving Germany had been the right decision—the only decision.

Peter's mother hugged me at the door. I could scarcely imagine her grief, since she and Elías had celebrated their fiftieth wedding anniversary the previous December, renewing their vows at their church, with friends and family bearing witness.

There were so many people at the Guzmán home, including Peter's extended family visiting from Mexico to be with Mica and to pray the rosary for her and Elías. I glanced back at Mica, and she seemed so small—barely five feet —rocking from foot to foot, and looking so alone that I went over and put my arm around her.

The photo of Elías with the wooden box containing his ashes seemed surreal. I kept expecting him to walk into the room. Even with all the evidence, his death didn't seem real. I didn't want it to be real.

Whenever Elías and I had spoken on the phone, we had gone through the same little ritual.

"How are you doing, Elías?" I'd ask.

"Well, still kickin'! I'm not dead yet," he'd reply. Then he would invite Peter and me to buy a big steak on him. Though we always promised we would, we only rarely had that steak.

What I most remembered about Elías was his generosity. He loved to garden, not for himself but so he would have vegetables to give away. He would shell the hundreds of walnuts that fell each year from his tree, somehow managing to create perfect little halves. I never liked walnuts until I tasted his—they were the best! He also sliced and dried the bounty from his fruit trees to give to fortunate folk like Peter and me.

At Elías's funeral, we saw how many people he had touched with his generosity and humour. Everyone had a special story, and it was a gift to hear about the Elías each had known. Since I'm not religious, being at church felt odd. I was crying my eyes out while trying not to, because I wanted the focus to be on Mica; Peter; his brother, Michael; and his sister, Vivian.

Leaving Peter to return to skating was difficult. I had to remind myself how proud Elías had been of my achievements. This brought to mind another realization: Though Peter had always supported me, this was the first time I had chosen Peter over sport, demonstrating to myself just how self-absorbed sport had encouraged me to be.

I did compete in the 2010 Olympic Games in Vancouver.

I did carry the flag in the Opening Ceremony.

I did win bronze in the 5000 metres, after one of the best races of my life.

When skier Kwame Nkrumah-Acheampong, nicknamed the "Snow Leopard," became the first Ghanaian ever to compete in a Winter Olympics, I could only imagine how stoked those kids in Ghana, to whom I had tried to explain snow, must have felt seeing him on TV. Kwame finished forty-seventh—second to last—in the slalom out of a starting field of 102, but at least he finished, whereas fifty-four did not. He proved to those kids in Ghana that anything is possible for those who strive and dream, just as Gaétan had shown me.

After my bronze-medal race, Peter and I became Olympic tourists—or tried to. I had never before had the level of recognition I received in Vancouver, and I never want to have it again. I was mobbed on the street. During the women's hockey final, people would ask for an autograph, or to take a photo. For a while it was cool, then I resorted to wearing a disguise.

The men's gold-medal hockey game was electric, almost explosive. During the Closing Ceremony, when Neil Young sang "Long May You Run," I was struck by the knowledge that a huge part of my life was over, leaving me with a mix of melancholy and relief.

As with other Olympics, I wanted to give something back. Before the Games, I'd taken that turn—the one where you find yourself on East Hastings, lost in a human wasteland of drunken, drugged people moving like zombies. Everywhere I went, I saw versions of how my life might have gone, if sport hadn't intervened. The contrast between East Hastings and the epic grandeur of the Olympic Games hit me hard. How could this be happening in the same city? Since we Canadian medal winners did receive bonuses in 2010, I donated my $10,000 to the Take a Hike program, an adventure-based learning initiative for at-risk youth. I had met some of those kids during the Games, and they were amazing.

I was also grateful to have made a connection with Joé Juneau, Team Canada's assistant *chef de mission,* whose stirring pre-Games pep talk had sent our national team into BC Place with a sense of purpose. As a former NHL player, Joé had enlisted Inuit kids in Nunavik, northern Quebec, into his Youth Hockey Development Programs. I had seen his students on TV, skating with the power and fluidity and toughness of warriors, despite lives overshadowed by alcoholism and poverty.

A few weeks after the Olympics, I went to Nunavik, where Joé urged me to share my story with Inuit students in the village of Kuu-jjuaq. I told kids in several classrooms how sport had saved me from my own confused youth, seeing in them the potential that others had seen in me. From there I flew to Kangiqsualujjuaq, an even smaller community on Ungava Bay. Though our plane held about twelve passengers, Kangiqsualujjuaq's airport lobby was jammed with people of every age. Babies' heads poked out of their moms' fur-trimmed hoods, with all hands stretched toward me. Each grip—sincere and intense— was matched with direct eye contact, warmly welcoming me into their hearts. The windows of the airport lobby were also packed with children's faces, stacked one atop the other, all smiling.

After the airport celebration, Andrea, a lovely young hockey player, escorted me to an awaiting dogsled. "Hold on tight!" she warned.

Soon we were sliding through the brooding mountains of the Canadian Arctic. Between shouts to the dogs in Inuktitut, Andrea asked me about the Olympics. Shouting back over all the yelping, I told her, "Nothing compares to this incredible moment, here, right now." I fell silent, drawing into myself the spectacular natural beauty surrounding me.

At the rink with Joé Juneau, I borrowed skates and a stick, then went on the ice with a bunch of kids of assorted ages. With each blast of the whistle, we took turns managing the puck or taking shots. I hadn't played on hockey skates in twenty years, and it showed, but none of that mattered. Once again, I saw how sport broke down barriers. As in Africa and in Gaza, so in the Canadian North.

The following day, I was escorted to the town's school, where I spoke to three groups of students, sharing my decades of experience in sport. They laughed at a classmate brave enough to try on my skin suit and racing glasses. They examined my speed skates and passed around my bronze medal from Vancouver. I was struck by how differently they handled it from other children. They palmed it, felt its weight and texture, rubbed the disc as if to polish it. I'd always felt my medals were meant to be shared, and I knew this one had more meaning after passing through those youthful Inuit hands.

Among the youngest girls, my red hair received almost as much attention as my medal. They asked to run their fingers through it, while the older students were content with handshakes, photos, and hugs.

I also told these kids about my difficulties growing up. I told them about my drinking in stairwells, my skipping school, and not caring about anything beyond making it through the day. It was harder talking about my immediate family—about my father's alcoholism and my sister's tragically dangerous life. Though these were memories I preferred to forget, I knew confession was the only way to reach through the wide eyes in front of me. I reminded these kids that life is precious and encouraged them to see that they could rise above hardship and despair to accomplish something worthwhile. I told them that being isolated from the urban resources of southern Canada didn't have to matter when it came to striving toward goals. What they had, and who they were, made them special.

Later, we returned to the rink for more hockey. We scrimmaged while rotating from bench to ice—passing, shooting, missing, and sometimes scoring. After an intense shift, I leaned my stick across my knees, then looked over at a boy less than half my size. He had positioned his stick exactly the same way as I had.

He smiled.

I caught my breath, then challenged, "Are you ready?"

He was. We played on.

These eager kids embodied the true Olympian spirit, or at least Joé's version. And they never seemed to tire.

I spent a night in a traditional Inuit camp reached during a whiteout. The floor of the canvas tent was spread with spruce bows, then caribou hides. A wood stove provided warmth as I gorged on fresh ptarmigan and char with my new friends.

I attended the start of a three-day hockey tournament the next morning, featuring players from twelve villages. The arena was packed with fans, bursting with a thrilling energy. Each player had earned the privilege of competing through school grades and good behaviour, not just through skill at hockey. The effectiveness of this selection process was demonstrated the first night of the tournament, when I was dining with Nancy Etok and Mark Brazeau, respectively the school's vice-principal and principal. At 8:00 P.M., a youth dropped off the late homework that had prevented him from playing during the day. After watching his friends skate without him, he'd hastily completed it so he could participate in that night's 10:45 game.

When I left for home, my luggage was packed with gifts presented to me throughout the week: a pair of *kamik*—traditional boots handmade by an elder named Christina; Inuit carvings and posters from the kids; a necklace symbolizing strength; caribou-skin mittens; and much more. However, the greatest, most lasting gifts were the intangible ones—the kindness and open hearts of the Inuit people who welcomed me into their world.

After Nunavik, I hit the speakers' circuit hard—fifty keynote speeches in eleven months. The downside was all the travel, as I was whisked from hotel to hotel, airport to airport: Moncton, Mississauga, Montreal, London, Ottawa, Calgary, Red Deer, Vancouver, and so on. Whenever I found time, I ran 20 to 30 kilometres to keep myself sane.

Since 2006, Bell Canada had been one of my sponsors, and after the Vancouver Games I received an invitation from Bell Canada Enterprises to go on the road with CEO George Cope to share my Olympic story with employees in major centres. When George mentioned that Bell was also launching a mental health initiative, I said, "I'd like to be involved." When he asked why, I told him about my dad and my sister, along with my own issues with depression. "I want to help change the system."

That piqued his interest.

In the summer of 2010, George and his wife, Tami, invited me to their home in Toronto, where they told me, "We'd like you to be the face of our initiative, if you're certain you won't be creating a bad situation with your family."

I replied, "I can talk about my own personal struggles, if that's enough."

They agreed it was.

I had no idea of the scope of my commitment, and to be honest, if I had, I'm not sure I would have agreed. At the same time, I felt compelled to work on the Bell Let's Talk campaign because I knew it would be useful for others with mental health issues to know what lay behind my well-publicized smile. Most people had no idea how different I truly was from my public persona, and some of that disconnect applied to me as well. I had never articulated to myself my whole story, only dealt with it in bits and pieces as emergencies arose. Explaining my life to others would allow me to learn about myself.

After committing to be the face of Bell's mental health initiative, I booked off the rest of the summer to kayak with Peter. We flew to Yellowknife, and though I'd never kayaked before, I had the audacity to think it was a skill I could pick up quickly. Not two hundred feet across Yellowknife Bay, the water was so rough I thought I was going to drown. While paddling as hard as I could, I shouted to Peter, "How could you put me out here? This is scary!" He shouted back: "If you think this is rough, you shouldn't be here."

Since Peter had spent months readying our gear for this trip, as well as selling our Calgary condo and moving us to a new home in Utah, he was already fed up with my griping.

When we arrived at a little rock island on Great Slave Lake, I was so stressed, not only from this trip but from all my speaking engagements, that I broke down in tears.

Peter flipped out on me. Even he has limits. "Okay, let's end this trip right here. This isn't working."

I fell asleep on the rock, and by the time I awoke, I'd calmed down. So had Peter. He asked me what I wanted to do. I replied, "Let's keep paddling."

It took us three weeks to reach Lutsel K'e, known both by its original Dene Chipewyan name and its English name, Snowdrift. After ending our kayaking trip at this fly-in village on the south shore of Great Slave Lake, we were invited to attend the annual Dene Chipewyan spiritual gathering. It would be held at Fort Reliance, near the Lady of the Falls, a sacred place of healing like Lourdes is for Catholics.

Peter and I spent five days sharing campfires, listening to drum dancing, and playing hand games. Peter helped cut wood for the sweat lodge fire and gather rocks to be heated all day in preparation. It was chokingly hot inside the sweat lodge. I crouched on my hands and knees in the dark, keeping close to the ground in order to breathe. The lodge reverberated with loud moaning, drumming, singing, the rattle of handmade shakers. The woman beside me dry-heaved for what seemed like hours, purging everything. This communal suffering was the closest I'd come to experiencing what it feels like to suffer when competing. Though our culture teaches us to avoid pain at all costs, I felt grateful for everything we shared at the gathering.

It was after the kayaking trip that I decided to act on a plan that had been brewing in my mind since 2008. I wanted to compete in the 2012 London Summer Olympics as a cyclist.

20
LONDON OLYMPICS 2012

Many people were surprised by my decision to enter the London Olympics. To my Order of Manitoba and my Order of Canada, I had now added a star on Canada's Walk of Fame in Toronto, as well as been inducted into Canada's Sports Hall of Fame. Wasn't enough enough?

In September 2006, I had been invited by CBC Sports to be a commentator for the World Cycling Championships in Salzburg, Austria. When I asked Xiuli for permission to skip some ice training, she responded with a big smile, "Clara, this is fantastic for your future. You should do this."

That's how I found myself at the 2006 World Championships, with a pair of running shoes as my only equipment, along with a four-day weight-training plan. Though television proved a tough learning experience, I'd never had so much fun at a Worlds. I wanted more.

I got that two years later at the Summer Olympics in Beijing. Once again, CBC invited me to talk about cycling. Those two summers, spent refilling my head with the excitement of bike racing, helped spur me toward London 2012. I'd long had the nagging feeling that I'd never been as good as I could have been on the bike, and I wanted to try again, after creating a positive training environment for myself.

After the Vancouver Games, Peter and I had moved from Calgary to an amazing house in Mount Aire Canyon, Utah, where I could live and train at high altitude. A narrow, 5-kilometre, one-lane mountain road led up from the interstate to the house situated at 7100 feet. The house is accessible in the snow season only by snowmobile. The views were phenomenal, and the area had abundant wildlife—moose, elk, bear, deer, bobcat, mountain lion. It was remote, yet only thirty-five minutes from an international airport. A big bonus for me was that, in the United States, I was totally anonymous.

Since I possessed a standing invitation to attend our national cycling camp, I went to the one held in Los Angeles in the summer of 2011. This, despite my having put on fifteen pounds eating bannock around campfires. When I asked coach Chris Rozdilsky if he'd be interested in working with me, he wrote a nine-page proposal about what he thought necessary to get me back into the sport. Chris was with the B2ten group, which funds athletes through donations. Though B2ten decided I wasn't in good enough shape for their pool of athletes, Chris told me, "Clara, we'll show them."

As for funding, I was grateful to receive the support of an anonymous donor, one of the first to match my $10,000 donation to RTP in 2006. When I happened to encounter him four years later in the Toronto airport lounge on my way to Rwanda for RTP, he volunteered to support anything I chose to do. "Just let me know how I can help." I contacted him with my plans for the London Summer Olympics, providing him with a budget for travel, for racing, coaching, and equipment. He generously granted me $90,000 a year for two years, simply to allow me to be the best I could be. All he asked in return was that I continue to set an example for Canada's youth.

My coaching relationship with Chris Rozdilsky proved a positive one. Chris was a very systematic and structured trainer, mirroring my experience with Xiuli in skating. Meanwhile, I was still making keynote speeches and busy in my first year of Bell Let's Talk. When I checked in to hotels to fulfill these commitments, I took my rollers with me.

One evening I was driving along a Quebec highway when I saw my face on an enormous billboard—one, then another, then another. At my Montreal training studio, everyone else had seen the billboards, too. Now that my public and private worlds had intersected, I found the questions disconcerting: "How can someone known for strength and joy have been depressed?"

I kept telling the two sides of my story, but it wore on me. The experience was truly much bigger than I had expected.

Three months after the Los Angeles training camp, I was back at the start line. While racing independently, I made the cut for the team pursuit, then competed at the World Track Cycling World Championships in Holland. That was when I decided the track was not for me. I was sick of going around in circles. I decided to focus on why I was on the bike again and what I really wanted to do: the time trial.

During that first year, while I was doing speed training, a coach rode ahead of me on her scooter, motor pacing me on the rural Ontario roads. I was drafting behind at 60 kilometres per hour when I hit a bump in the road, which sent me flying forward onto the hard asphalt. My head bounced off the pavement, splitting my helmet. My BlackBerry in my back pocket saved half of my back from road rash, though it was ground into dust by the impact.

In the 2011 World Championships in Denmark, I was in a solo breakaway that lasted for the second half of the road race but was caught by the peloton with only 2 kilometres to go. Moments later, I was tangled in a heap of bodies and bikes, reminding me how easily this sport brings a rider to her knees. One minute you're almost the world champion, the next you're sprawled on your back with another broken-boned cyclist on top of you.

During the second year of my cycling comeback, 2012, I signed with the team Specialized-lululemon. We were to ride in Belgium's Flèche Wallonne Femmes, infamous for its relentless three-tier climb, with the Mur de Huy as its crowning glory. The Mur de Huy, or Wall of Huy, is a steep hill with vertical stretches that create panic attacks. I had ridden the Flèche back in 1998, when I was thirteen years younger. After my teammate Sue Palmer had described it to me, I remember thinking: *It can't be that bad.* But it was. My wildest imaginings couldn't have mirrored its terrible reality. It opened a wound, rubbed in salt, then laughed in my face as I burned with pain.

In a pre-race meeting, our directeur sportif, Ronny Lauke, gave Trixi Worrack, Evie Stevens, Amber Neben, Ally Stacher, Emilia Fahlin, and me our tasks. Mine was hard to believe:

1. Climb over the damn Mur, either with the front group or just behind.
2. Get with the leaders, wasting no energy, because the real work would soon begin.
3. ATTACK!

As Trixi explained, "Just sit up and get over the Mur. Don't try to lead or chase. You sit, and let others do the work. You save your energy, and when your instinct tells you it's time, you attack."

That's all? Attack, when every cell in my body told me I'd be lucky to make it up the Mur with the stragglers?

I went to the start with more than 150 others. Massive winds, bouts of rain, crashes, a peloton wipeout caused by a motorcycle. Twists, turns, hills, towns, forests, big roads and small, bumps, loose gravel. We mad female cyclists—a storming chaos—made our way through the Belgian countryside.

Starting the Mur at the front helped. I let riders go by me, then wove back into the group of accelerating women who were passing and re-passing and blowing up. It was like being in a video game, except I was in full control of how I chose to manoeuvre. I made it up the Mur as my teammates said I would, about twenty seconds behind the leaders, strong and ready to attack.

I sat and let others chase because I had three teammates ahead in that group of twenty-five. Three teammates—Trixi, Evie, and Amber—who were waiting for me to make the move that would start our race. My other two teammates—Ally and Emilia—had already done a superb job, safely positioning us at the foot of the Mur. Now it was my turn—task number 3. A slew of riders were anticipating my attack, so I had to wait. Sit and float. I felt the moment, and I was off.

The last 30 kilometres of that race will be forever etched in my memory. While I hammered my way ahead, the three climbing machines who were my teammates sat and spun their legs back in the peloton. Then, with approximately 6 kilometres to go, Dutch superstar Marianne Vos bridged the gap till she was only about 50 feet behind me. I could see Evie parked on her wheel. Evie's style is unmistakable. She rides like she's bopping to a hit tune on her iPod. I knew the critical moment was approaching. I was tired, with the wind blowing from all directions, but I pounded two GU gels from my pocket, took a swig of Coke that I'd grabbed from the feed station above the Mur, then told myself: *Now go!*

I didn't say a word to Evie. No words were necessary. I just rode as hard as I could for the next 5.4 kilometres, with Vos sitting behind me, and the sounds of suffering roaring out of me. All I knew was that I had to bring Evie to the Mur so she—*we!*—could win.

Halfway up the second climb of the Mur, Evie looked at me for a signal. I yelled: "Be smart!"

Evie smiled, nodded, and rode away.

I was proud that I didn't fall off my bike. I grunted, using every fibre of muscle to keep my pedals turning.

Evie won in spectacular fashion. I held on for eighth place, knowing we'd won as a team. We cheered like goofy kids.

The Flèche Wallonne Femmes was a high point of my 2012 cycling renaissance. It was an additional thrill to donate all the money I made from cycling that year to RTP to fund Mali's Youth Initiative.

My road to the 2012 Olympics, held in London from July 25 to August 12, was fraught with more difficulties.

After winning the time trial in the Grand Prix Cycliste Gatineau, I crashed the following day in the road race. A young triathlete, who was trying to make the Olympic team, was a bad technical rider, and not very smart about it. I was stupid enough to be on her wheel in a tight turn, and when she took herself out, I went into her. My bike flipped over my back, and my bike saddle nailed me directly in the spine.

I refused to accept this young woman's apology. Still seething, I picked up her bike and threw it at her. I'm not proud of that, but it happened. Fortunately, I missed her, but the bike ricocheted off the road, nearly taking out a few of my teammates in the pack. Still not finished, I yelled: "Get the fuck away from me before I do something I regret!"

The officials didn't see me, but I deserved to be disqualified. All I could think was: *She injured my back! Badly*. And it was late May, two months before the Games.

I remounted, then made it to the front of the pack, where I tried to help my Specialized-lululemon teammate Ina Teutenberg win, but I was in too much pain. As I lay on my back in our minivan, icing my injury, I still couldn't believe what had happened. Though I'm ashamed of myself to this day, I still couldn't apologize to that triathlete. She shouldn't have been competing but then again, women's cycling allows that sort of thing.

Gatineau, Quebec, was another place in which my two lives—cyclist and mental health advocate—meshed.

I first met Luke Richardson, a former NHL player, and his wife, Steph, when I dropped the puck at an Ottawa Senators game dedicated to youth mental health awareness. The Richardsons' vibrant and athletic daughter, Daron, had taken her own life at the age of fourteen. Their grief over this incredible loss, along with the outpouring of sorrow from Daron's friends, led to a powerful desire to *do* something, which found its expression in a youth mental health awareness program called Do It for Daron (DIFD), for which Steph and Luke raised millions of dollars.

I felt proud that I had been wearing the purple DIFD bracelet the previous year in the Grand Prix Cycliste Gatineau, when I won the time trial but lost the road race, and again in 2012, when I also won the time trial but crashed in the road race.

I was at the Richardsons' home when I received a call for a random doping test, to which Steph volunteered to drive me. Despite testing positive for reasons still unknown in Sicily back in 1994, I had by now taken so many doping tests that I was capable of seeing the humour in them.

While I was training in Calgary for the Vancouver Olympics, two very polite women from CCES (Canadian Centre for Ethics in Sport) had arrived at my condo at 7:55 P.M., read me my rights along with the notice of testing, then filled out the proper forms. I have, by the way, a bunch of towels and T-shirts, long-sleeved and short-, with the CCES emblem, boldly stating their intention for drug-free sports.

I chugged a few sealed bottles of water, told them I was ready to go, then went into the bathroom with one of them following. Because I, as any athlete, take this peeing in a cup as a competition, just like everything else I do, I planned to complete it as fast as I could. My record for the whole deal—paperwork, peeing, bottling, signing—is about seven minutes, a personal best I'm proud of.

Just as I was ready to pee—in full view of the chaperone, whose job it was to "watch the stream of urine leave the body and enter the cup"— she decided to chat, possibly to cover her own awkwardness, which I, as a pro, didn't share: "So, only one year!"

"Only one year to what?" I asked.

"The Olympics, of course. You must be excited!"

But excited was not what I was feeling at that moment. I said, "I don't think about it too much," distracting myself sufficiently to miss the cup, spilling the valuable contents. I had to wait another ten minutes before I could—by trying really, really hard—produce another half ounce.

But that was then, this is now: I'm happy to say that on the doping test in Gatineau, I was able to perform to perfection.

The day after my crash in the Grand Prix Cycliste Gatineau, I flew on schedule to Idaho to compete in a stage race with my pro team, Specialized-lululemon, but I couldn't even put on my socks. I couldn't pull on my skin suit or dismount from my bike. As the days went by, brushing my teeth and using a fork with my right hand became impossible. Then, hours before the Idaho race, I crashed yet again, adding whiplash to my undiagnosed back injuries.

After I returned home to Utah, I called my mentor Hubert Lacroix, whose brother, Vincent, was an orthopedic surgeon and head doctor for the Montreal Canadiens. After having secured an appointment with Dr. Lacroix, I flew to Montreal.

With my speed skating coach Xiuli Wang at the Salt Lake City Olympics, 2002

Winning bronze in women's 5000-metre speed skating at the 2002 Olympics

Racing at the 2006 Torino Olympics *(The Canadian Press)*

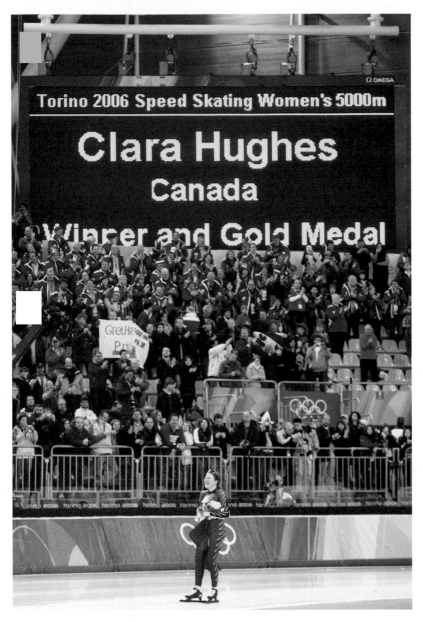

Winning gold in women's 5000-metre speed skating at the
2006 Torino Olympics (*Getty Images*)

Named an Honorary Quebec Athlete with Premier Jean Charest
after the 2006 Olympics (*Quebec government*)

Joining in the fun with Right to Play in Ethiopia, 2006

Winning bronze in women's
5000-metre speed skating at
the 2010 Vancouver Olympics
(*The Canadian Press*)

Hugging Mom after winning bronze at the 2010 Olympics

Receiving the Order of Canada from Governor General Michaëlle Jean, 2010
(*The Canadian Press*)

Canada's Walk of Fame, 2010
(*The Canadian Press*)

In the wind tunnel testing my aerodynamics for the 2012 Olympic time trial

Celebrating my thirty-ninth birthday in the Utah desert with Peter, 2011

With Joé Juneau and members of the
Nunavik Youth Hockey Development Program, 2010

With an amazing Dene elder, Madeline Catholique, in Great Slave Lake, 2010

With Mom at Sydenham Hill, renamed Clara's Climb, in Dundas, Ontario, 2013

An MRI confirmed what he had previously diagnosed: The spinous process had been snapped off from my seventh thoracic vertebra, sometimes called the T7. The spinous process is the bony projection on each vertebra where spinal muscles and ligaments are attached. In short, I had a broken back.

Dr. Lacroix assured me that the break was a superficial one, and that I wouldn't further damage myself by racing. But that still didn't explain the source of my excruciating pain.

I called my osteopath in France—Benoit Nave, the most incredible therapist on earth. He told me to lie on my stomach so that Peter could examine my back. He instructed Peter to count down my vertebrae to the break at number seven. Then he asked, "Does it look twisted?"

It did.

Benoit said, "Your T6 has locked up to protect the impact zone. Unless someone unlocks it, the pain will continue."

Before I could do anything about this, I had to race the Olympic trials, which I won. Then I flew to France so Benoit could work on my back. In one adjustment, the pain was gone. Benoit treated me again in France, in Italy, and then in London, just to make sure my T6 stayed unlocked.

During all this time, I was troubled by more than my injury. After ten years away from cycling as a sport, I'd become terrified to ride in the rain. I always imagined my wheels were sliding from under me, so that I became unsettled whenever clouds gathered, or a weather report forecast inclement weather. An inner voice kept warning me: *Remember Nicole? You could die doing this, you know.*

It didn't help that the 2012 Olympics were being staged in a city known for rain.

The theme of the London XXX Olympiad was "Inspire a Generation." The number of participating nations was 204, with 10,568 athletes and 302 events in 26 sports. As head of state for the host country, Queen Elizabeth II presided over the Opening Ceremony.

Naturally, the dark skies gathered on the day of my road race. We were to start and finish on the Mall, the street running to Buckingham Palace, with loops in and around Surrey. I went straight to the front and stayed there, till the wet roads stirred my dread, wasting my energy. When the winning breakaway took off, I was there, but I lacked the power to go with it. I ended up a dismal thirty-second.

In the time trial, I felt good, but not great, and I finished fifth. When Coach Chris and I studied my power output from the bike's SRM—a device that records the power for every ounce of energy put into the pedal stroke—I found that it was my best ride ever. My great performance wasn't good enough. Four cyclists had been better.

Afterward, when the media questioned me, I made no excuses. I said, "Well, I was beaten, but I couldn't have raced any better." I also added, "That's it, guys. Now I'm done."

Later, I told Peter, "I don't think I ever realized until that moment how really hard it is to win an Olympic medal."

What was important to me was that I'd lost well. Losing, yet feeling good about the race, was still a new experience for me, and one I believe to be a metaphor for life. Though our culture puts great emphasis on winning, the rewards we think we want aren't necessarily what we need. I also realized, for the very first time, that no matter what I did—whether I won or lost a race—it would have no real impact on the guilt and need and fear and self-hatred that I'd been dragging around with me since my childhood. Suddenly, it was all very clear: That was a war I would have to fight on open ground.

After the time trial, Peter and I stayed in London for a few days. We saw U.S. swimmer Michael Phelps capture his fourth gold medal, making him the most decorated Olympic athlete of all time, with a medal count of twenty-two.

By then, both Peter and I had had enough.

We flew to Geneva, where we rented a car, then stopped in a village for pizza and wine. Since a festival was taking place, we couldn't find a room, so we simply pulled off the main road. From a London five-star hotel, we'd downscaled to sleeping in a little rented car. When I woke up, I was startled to discover my feet had swollen like balloons. This was the result of yet another pair of extremes. After my strict training diet, I had gone straight to eating butter, fat, and salt. That realization didn't stop me from enjoying some good-morning croissants though.

Peter and I ended up in Argentière, a picturesque mountaineering village in the Mont Blanc area. We hiked, picked wild blueberries, and searched for chanterelle mushrooms. Then, on August 12, the day of the London Closing Ceremony, we found ourselves in a small pizzeria in Argentière. After meeting the proprietor and his wife, we asked if they would mind putting on the Games. While I was in the washroom, Peter told them why. My cover was blown, but it was okay, because they were excited to be hosting us.

After returning to North America, Peter and I hiked the John Muir Trail in California. I did a lot of trail running—100 kilometres a week. I also travelled to the village in Uganda featured on the Right to Play documentary I had seen at the Torino Olympics. This allowed me to thank the Ugandan RTP coaches and staff for helping me win a gold medal, which I showed to them. I told them they'd inspired someone an ocean away, and that I never would have been able win without them. Most profoundly, I was able to meet with children, like those I'd seen the morning of my race, who had transformed my Olympian struggle into joy.

Back home once again, I was very busy fulfilling commitments for Bell Let's Talk. But then came winter.

LIVING IN A PERMANENT OFF-SEASON

21

THAT BILLBOARD SMILE

So, now it was over. Really over.

After the London Olympics, I thought everything would be much easier. That last hurrah had felt like an exploration of the self rather than a race—a milestone in inner discovery that had taught me what was important. Now I could be a "normal" person, living a balanced life, without the pressures rooted in racing. Why not? I had money in the bank, a supportive husband, and a successful career that had provided me with enough celebrity to build a future. For a couple of months—maybe even three—all that made sense. Then the question of *what now?* set in.

I started to feel that familiar darkness rising like a suffocating fog from some hopeless place inside me. Without recognizable goals, my old negative thought patterns became stronger—patterns of self-punishment that screamed loudest whenever I sat too long with myself. This nagging abuse began to follow me into my time with others, so that I created a cloud of misery wherever I went. That billboard smile wasn't working for me anymore. Or for anyone else.

Though I'd often had frightening glimpses of a deeper truth, I'd insisted on believing my toxic inner chatter was the result of striving to be better at something difficult. That something was sport, which had consumed me for over two decades but was no more. Now I faced no pressures of training and competing. No need to be fast, good, or strong. I had no daily goals beyond personal satisfaction, whatever that was. Ironically, the demands I had blamed for my dissatisfaction I now blamed, in their absence, for my depression. I couldn't go back, I didn't want to go back. The part of me that had found release, satisfaction, purpose through competition was exhausted. All I wanted was to find pleasure in each day, to enjoy the continuing gift of a strong body, the glories of nature, and Peter's companionship. What I hadn't factored in was the one constant before and after sport: me. Without the distraction of busyness, "I" could no longer be avoided.

A neighbour who was a former athlete described retirement as living in a permanent off-season. That's exactly how I felt. For an athlete, it takes creativity and discipline to be sedentary. When I was still racing, I used to find it easy, after months of intensive training, to occupy downtime by cleaning, shovelling, reading, or relaxing in front of a fire with a fresh cup of espresso. For a few days. Then I began itching inside my skin, aching for some kind of structure, yearning for the monotony of having something to do . . . anything but nothing. That's when I would begin "improving" the house, resulting in frustration—usually for Peter, who ended up completing my projects.

When we lived in Quebec, I tried yoga, available in Sutton, 20 kilometres away. I found it hard to sit. Difficult to relax and stretch. Eventually, I did tune out and tune in. Until the chanting began, with misty-eyed participants rocking back and forth in creative versions of the lotus position. Then they lost me. All I could do was sit and stretch my neck, intrigued by these entranced women, chanting foreign words, loud and strong. I felt happy for them, but of course, I didn't need any of it. I had sport . . . most of the time.

I went back to chopping wood, finding peace in the monotony of demolishing stump after stump, focusing on hitting the perfect place where the wood naturally cracked. *Chop-chop-chop. Calm.*

So, while I had rehearsed "retirement" during previous off-seasons, I hadn't been good at it. I had made it through, though, knowing my "real" life would soon begin. On the bike. On skates. Now, I was sidelined forever. The days, the weeks, the months stretched before me, during which I stayed inside far too much, and that's when the unanswerable questions hit me hardest: *What does it matter if you never go for another bike ride, or put on your skates again? Who cares?* Followed by accusations creeping in: *Why are you so tired when you don't do anything? Why aren't you out on your bike, your skates, climbing a mountain, hiking a trail? Aren't those activities you're supposed to like?*

If I replied: *I've retired,* the sneering response would be: *Then, what's the point of your life?* Or: *What's the point of those medals you won?*

Such questions circulated like grit through the soft tissue of my mind, preventing transformation, or even a bit of fun. Some of these I thought I'd dealt with throughout the years, but now that I had all day, every day, to be vulnerable, my piecemeal solutions didn't provide me with enough armour to protect me from those inner demons. The drumbeat of self-accusation, at war with the seeds of peace trying to take root, eventually coalesced into one devastating message: *Clara, you aren't good enough. You've never been good enough, and nothing you've ever done has changed that.*

That idea began to eat me alive. *Not good enough.* It was scary. Until I could respond in a meaningful way, nothing else mattered.

In some ways, being a former athlete is like being an addict. After retirement, it's easy to remember the big wins and to forget the torture. Just like the alcoholic or the druggie, you dwell on the highs, while repressing thoughts of the morning after. You yearn for another big hit, resulting in melancholy when you realize your other life is over.

In retrospect, I believe my dysfunctional family life had helped me succeed at the Olympic level. I was able to channel my tolerance for extremes into sport, pushing myself to places I shouldn't have been able to go. It fed my desire to win and never be satisfied with my last high. I couldn't take a day off without clubbing myself with guilt, and when I wasn't racing, I was compulsively yearning for my next fix.

The extreme physical pain I was able to endure was a distraction from my emotional pain. I was like a traumatized person who slashes open a vein with a razor to let the despair, the guilt, the repressed anger bleed out. I would cut myself to the bone, grinding and hammering before I'd give up. That was why Mirek, with his aggressive coaching, was such a great fit for me. It was only after winning two bronze medals in the Atlanta Olympics that I came to the stark realization that perhaps medals weren't going to provide me with self-worth. That's when the depression began again, and the self-abuse, sometimes with alcohol, sometimes with food. Even silver and gold hadn't helped.

During my decades as a professional athlete, a line of mentors and supporters had provided some awareness of, even fleeting relief from, my inner chaos. All my coaches—Peter Williamson, Mirek Mazur, Eric Van den Eynde, Xiuli Wang, and Chris Rozdilsky—had been authority figures. All but Mirek had provided some support against my unsettling childhood.

In 1997 our national team doctor had dared to mention the word *depression* to me. Though I flew into a frenzy of denial, she had slid open a dreaded door I knew someday I might have to open.

When I returned to skating, I was aided by Cal Botterill, a sports psychologist to whom I spoke for the first time about my off-season struggles to find peace. He helped me in my developmental years as an athlete to understand that the belief I was a failure was not rooted in reality. However, since I was still racing, my "solution" was to train harder: *Be better, be stronger.*

Terry Orlick, another sports psychologist, made me aware of the process I used to channel energy for my biggest races. Before Terry, I was afraid to wade into those waters because "it just happened." Then I began to ask myself: *What if it doesn't "just happen"?*

Terry sent me a list of everything I'd said to him, over the course of a few discussions, organized clearly and in point form, effectively showing me how I made my mind work for me. I was surprised when I read the list: *That's me? That's cool!* The list is almost a mantra:

- If you don't focus in the moment, you won't live your goals and dreams. But at some point, dream goals and realistic goals can merge.
- Turn fear into focus
- Doubts into focus
- Disappointment/setbacks into focus
- What focus is going to help you right now?

Every day ask yourself: What am I going to do today to take myself one step closer to my goals and dreams?

You can only live this day once, this opportunity now. Once it is gone, it is gone. Embrace the opportunity.

Appreciate what you have already accomplished:

- Your own qualities
- Your personal victories
- Qualities in your teammates
- Qualities in coaches and support staff
- Family/meaningful relationships
- People who care
- People who helped you get here
- People who are helping you get better
- The beautiful places you train, race, visit
- The opportunities you have

When I read over this list, I knew it spoke to more than racing, but I wasn't ready to turn it into a mantra of renewal for my off-season life.

One sports psychologist actually thought it was helpful to arrive inconveniently on my doorstep and hand me a teddy bear. At that time I was living in the Calgary condo Peter and I had purchased. I heard a knock on our door, reached from an outside patio. I didn't want to let the person in, but it was freezing outside. When I answered, the response was, "Clara, I just wanted to make sure you were feeling okay, and I brought you a present."

While I appreciated the intention, I hate stupid, useless gestures. It felt disingenuous hearing about an event with various A-listers, while I strangled the teddy bear. The member of our support staff had no idea what was going on inside of me, but it was this person's job. Instead of feeling the support I needed, I had to waste energy avoiding this person.

Dr. David Smith, my skating physiologist, described this type of approach as the J-Squared syndrome, defined as "job justification," applicable to staff who felt the need to be seen working with their athletes. Doc Smith was always up in the stands, invisible unless you wanted him. Then, all of a sudden, he'd be beside you. Though he helped build my confidence, his job for Team Canada—like those of the sports psychologists—was to make me a better machine so I could win races, especially every four years at the Olympics.

I received my most personal insights from those outside the system. In 2000 I sent Peter to Winnipeg to meet my family and to watch the Sydney Olympics with them. I didn't explain the Hughes dynamics because . . . what was there to explain? We were a normal family, right?

He met my parents at our Elmwood house, where he witnessed how meanly my dad treated my mom. After that, he watched my first race with my dad. Dad was drunk and spent his time belittling my sister. Despite Dodie's issues, Peter thought she was doing her best, but my dad kept relentlessly beating her down.

Peter camped in a provincial park to get away from my family, then left days later to watch the rest of the Olympics with friends in Kenora. Afterward he asked, "How could you have suggested that? Don't ever do that to me again."

"What do you mean?"

He described what had happened, adding, "Your sister is such a champ."

I wasn't ready to hear any of this, so I was angry at Peter, but he had given me a realistic yardstick for judging what was "normal," which I would eventually trust: *My family is dysfunctional? So that's what that word means!*

When I was presented with the Order of Manitoba in 2006, I was given another of those yardsticks. My mom brought my dad to the big awards dinner at the Manitoba legislature, even though they were divorced. As usual, my dad got drunk and started disparaging her. When other guests at the table exchanged knowing looks, I was mortified at having put my mom in that humiliating situation. However, it wasn't until my dad had a temper tantrum in the parking lot that I realized: *Mom is being abused.*

My massage therapist, Shayne Hutchins, who was interested in alternative medicine, gave me a great gift one day in 2007 when he told me: "You know, I'm working with a Calgary energy doctor whom you should see. He's also a physician. He's a weird dude—you'll either love him or never want to go back."

So, I made an appointment to see Dr. Owen Schwartz, who practised out of an ugly building on Sixteenth Avenue. He greeted me in his waiting room, all decorated purple with crystals. "Clara, nice to meet you." His hair was wild, and one eye looked sideways. Clearly hippie trippy. Clearly out there. But wasn't that why I was here?

I followed Dr. Schwartz into his office, where I suddenly started talking about things I'd never shared with anyone—how shitty I felt inside, my issues with food, my sense of being surrounded by selfish people who took advantage, the toxic environment of sports, my dad and his drinking, my sister's illness, my mom and her difficult life.

As Owen came to know me, he said, "Clara, the gift you have for others is just being present. You offer an example of focus, of dedication, of intensity. You don't need to give any more than that. If you choose to help someone, ask yourself if that person is going to pass on your gift. If so, maybe it's worthwhile. If not, just be there, be you, and realize that's enough."

His words reinforced what Xiuli had been telling me for years. "Clara, you need to be careful to whom you open your heart, because some people don't belong inside and some do, and you need to know the difference."

Owen was the first person to tell me that just being "me" was enough. This was such an epic realization that it allowed me to continue training, day in and day out, taking me through that difficult time from Torino to Vancouver.

After a number of sessions, Owen suggested that I try regression therapy to deal with my overwhelming feelings of guilt about the unhappiness in my family. "I'm not going to hypnotize you, but I'll guide you back into your past. It's different for every person, but I think it's worth a try if you're interested."

I agreed. I remember lying down on Owen's examining table, closing my eyes, then hearing his soothing voice: "Go back in time, back to Clara as a young athlete, as a teenager. Now, I want you to return to the first time you felt helpless, to that very real place where everything was out of your control."

I began to feel as if I actually was somewhere else.

"Do you see yourself?"

"Yes, I'm a little girl."

"Do you know where you are?"

"I'm in my family house. I'm standing in the area behind the kitchen."

"Do you hear anything?"

"I hear my mom and dad."

"What time of day is it?"

"It's night, and my dad has just come home. My mom has set out his dinner, and he's telling her everything is wrong with it. He's yelling at her. He's drunk. My mom is standing there, not saying anything."

"What are you doing?"

"I'm sitting, or maybe I'm standing."

"What are you feeling?"

"I want the angry sounds to stop. I want my dad to stop yelling at my mom, but I can't make him stop!"

"Is anyone with you right now?"

"I'm alone."

"Look around you. Do you see anything at all?"

I found myself staring at my finger. "I see a bird. It's sitting on my finger." I actually did feel the weight of that bird. It was so strange.

"What is the bird doing?"

"It's looking at me."

"How is it looking at you?"

"With loving eyes."

"How do you feel when you look at that bird?"

"I feel relief, because it's telling me with its eyes that everything is okay, and that I'm going to be okay."

"What's happening now?"

"I'm smiling at the bird."

"I want you to look at your mom, and I want you to tell her that you love her, but that you can't rescue her, and that you can't fix what's happening between her and your father."

I looked at my mom, and I told her those things. She didn't look at me, but I heard my own words.

Owen continued, "I want you to look at your dad and tell him the same thing."

I did as Owen said. I told my dad that I loved him, but I couldn't fix him or rescue him from his problems.

"Look back at the bird. What is happening now?"

"The bird is smiling at me."

At that point, I started coming out of the trance, or whatever it was, and I remember feeling I was suddenly physically present with Owen, after my having been alone in that other space.

Owen said, "Clara, take as much time as you need to return to this reality. If there's anything you want to say, say it now, or just be still within yourself."

I started laughing. "I feel as if my heart is enormous. I feel possessed by this huge, huge heart, and I feel so free, and I feel so good."

Then I opened my eyes. "Oh, that was weird!"

Owen confirmed, "You went back, and you were able to be that kid in that difficult situation, and now I want you to take the words you said to your mom and dad, and I want you to live them. You cannot rescue either of them. They are who they are, and now you are free to be who you are."

The regression treatment was one of the most powerful experiences I've ever had, and it left me better equipped to return home to Winnipeg. That was when I ended for good the insanity of family get-togethers in which everything went to hell. Instead, I would tell my mom and my grandmother, my dad and my sister, "Okay, I have two days, and I want to see you all, but not at the same time."

In this way, I could love each one, deal with each one, then leave each one. I established control over my visits that I didn't have as a child. I also realized that, since I was the one who had escaped, my coming home often made everything worse. My guilt didn't completely disappear, but at least I had a handle on it.

As for that little messenger bird . . . it reminded me of the flute-voiced wood thrush that had remained hidden from Peter and me until the day we decided to get married—our wedding bird, bringing me back to the peace of Glen Sutton.

Unexpectedly it also took me back to a powerful piece of art by the Ojibway artist Jackson Beardy. A brilliantly coloured woodpecker possessing a huge head and eyeballs so big they seemed about to explode. Its beak pierced the earth, sucking out life, like the continuing cycle of birth and death. I knew that some important healing had taken place that day, but then I became distracted again. I was still racing.

22

LET THE BEAUTIFUL TEARS FLOW

Not long after my retirement, Peter and I were watching a documentary about a videographer who had been killed in Libya. I could feel the tears forcing their way out, but I closed my eyes tightly because I didn't want to cry. Here I was, sitting in my own living room. Here I was, with my own husband. Here I was, watching a story about the death of someone whom we both liked, yet I was holding back my tears.

After all these years, I was still the kid in the closet, too frightened to cry over something I couldn't control.

Suddenly, I remembered Tewanee Joseph's brushing-off ceremony before the Vancouver Olympics. I remembered how his thirteen-year-old daughter had stood before us, unselfconsciously crying her heart out, and how the elder had said, "Thank you for sharing your beautiful tears with us. Let them flow."

In that moment, I understood that, to rescue the part of me still locked in that closet, I would have to admit my vulnerability. I would have to let my beautiful tears flow. I also sensed that I would need help.

I began to make inquiries. I learned that the Canadian Sport Centre in Calgary provided funding for athletes for five years after retirement to help them transition from sport. That was how I found clinical psychologist Hap Davis. Hap not only specialized in depression and anxiety among athletes but also worked with street people, addicts, abused women, and refugees.

When Hap and I first met, I sat in his office and cried. After that, everything was on the table—issues with food, my sense of failure, guilt over my successes, and so on. This regular outlet with Hap, during which I could talk without judgement while being offered concrete advice, provided a wonderful release.

Bell Let's Talk also put me in contact with Dr. David Goldbloom, a psychiatrist and senior medical adviser for Toronto's Centre for Addiction and Mental Health. Both Hap and David offered professional support with no strings attached. No one was trying to make me faster and better. It was all about how I felt.

One of the gifts both gave me was their understanding—far deeper than my own—of the trauma I had endured as a child. I told David about it pretty openly, and it was a relief to have him acknowledge how tough things had been for me.

Hap confirmed this in his pseudo-jocular way. "You're depressed? No kidding! What a surprise."

For the first time, I let myself accept that I, as a child, had suffered through really dark, painful situations that were not my fault, leaving a powerful residue against which I had struggled all of my adult life. I recognized that I still carried an ocean of grief inside of me, some of it held back for so long that I no longer knew the cause. My warrior self had served me well while I was competing in the arena. Now, I needed to have the courage to accept my wounded self.

I also had anger issues to own and to confront. As a kid, I felt safer being angry like my father than submissive and vulnerable like my mother. My anger helped me survive. Now that I was an adult, it also helped me deal with some of the unfairness in competitive sport, be my own person, and set my own course. But outside of the arena, this anger had become a heavy burden for me and for others, especially for Peter. For no good reason, I would turn into this volatile, raging person who needed a target—anyone or anything—to release the lava from my internal volcano. Even today, I'm still learning how to deal with these outbursts. Now, however, when I feel a surge of rage, I'm more capable of stopping myself with the reminder: *You're no longer a kid at risk. Don't be this uncontrolled monster. Don't turn into the abusive part of your dad. Every issue isn't about survival.*

When my temper is triggered by a situation that involves Peter, I know in my heart that he is an incredibly decent person who always does his best, even if it isn't exactly what I want. And what, exactly, do I want? I don't always know. I'm not necessarily right or wrong, nor is he. We may just have different viewpoints.

It comes back to my realizing, as often as necessary, that my over-the-top rage is just the result of my peeling down through the layers and years of mistrust and unfairness that I couldn't deal with as a child. Now, as an adult, I have a choice: I can continue to let that anger drive me into a really bad place, or I can take a step back to view the situation from a broader perspective. I can choose instead to embrace the beauty and the love that are all around me. It's ironic how much easier it is to be charming, fun, and caring to strangers—to be that smiling person on the billboard—than to be positive and tolerant to those who are always there for me, who truly love me. That's a whole different level of being, and the place where I find myself more often now.

Another lesson I'm learning in retirement is balance. This means going with a mid-level flow, not hyping my emotions to such an un-natural high that I eventually have to come tumbling down. I've also reached a stage in my life when I can enjoy spaces in which nothing is happening, and even seek them out. When I was in my *doing-doing-doing* phase, I crashed because all that busyness wasn't sustainable. While my version of "nothing" might mean going on a 500-kilometre hike, or climbing a mountain, or just strolling through the woods, these are ac-tivities that I can now enjoy on their own merits. They have nothing to do with distracting me from my negative feelings, or training me for some future achievement. Many of my goals today are small and invisible to others. Goals like changing the words inside my head to express happier thoughts. Goals of identifying a new bird or discovering an exciting book. Goals of standing still instead of moving like a freight train through life's wonderful moments, forgetting to experience their enchantment.

I still have times when I feel a harsh sense of self-loathing, especially when winter chills my bones. I begin to hate myself. I hate everything I am, and everything I say. I feel ugly and awful and stupid—a fat clump of worthless nothing.

That phrase "fat clump" connected to "worthless" shows I still have issues with food and body image. When I was a kid, a boy said to me, "One day you'll be fat." It was as if he had injected me with a venom that poisoned my thoughts for decades to come. This is not unique to me. So many women have had experiences like that, thanks to a culture addicted to thinness.

Food disorders are especially prevalent among females in power sports. Not only are we on public display but the necessity to build muscles sometimes undermines our sense of femininity. It's even more complicated than that. In competitive sport, control enters into everything we do. Manipulating the body through food restriction starts out feeling like a good thing: *I'm in control of my engine.* At the same time, the conflict between lightness for speed and muscle for power creates an unsolvable problem. While competing, I felt good about myself when I ate very little, no more than 800 calories a day, preferably nothing at all. Being unable to sustain that goal made me feel like a failure, made me want to eat more, causing more guilt. And my battle was reinforced by my teammates, who were striving after the same false and dangerous goals.

I still have trouble knowing what I look like, which isn't an image problem limited to women in sport. I see pictures of myself and I think: *Is that me?* If I look fat, I beat myself up. If I seem slender, I have trouble connecting with that reality because of the enormous emotional weight I'm carrying. If a friend says, "Look at your legs, they're beautiful," I'll say, "Really?" because I can't see what impressed her. I still struggle with what I see in the mirror. Sometimes I'm totally at peace with myself and I feel beautiful, but too often I do not.

Unlike alcohol or drugs or other addictive substances, food isn't something you can just give up, though I certainly tried. I loved to cook with my father. I love to cook with Peter. Cooking is a happy thread running through my life. I envy people who are indifferent to food, along with those who can stop eating when they're full. Some can even forget to have a meal. Both Peter and I love to eat. Though we can easily overdo it, Peter doesn't struggle the way I do. I don't have a reliable shutoff valve. I can eat as long as food is available. That's not about nourishment. That's addiction. I'm trying to train myself to leave the table a little hungry. I'm trying to think of food as a life-giving gift. I'm also trying to resist exercising more just so I can eat more.

Hap always reminds me, "You know this isn't really about food. The issue is much more deeply rooted. If we deal with it from that deeper place, everything will sort itself out."

I have to agree with him, because when I am clear and open about self-value, food ceases to be an issue. Then, I do enjoy eating, and I do know when to stop. That really good place lasts for a spell, till darker feelings creep in. The difference now is that I know when I need help, when I need to talk, to articulate. It's when I internalize that nasty voice, letting it take over, that I get into trouble.

In examining my family's multi-generational history of alcoholism and other emotional problems, it's fair to assume that I'm genetically predisposed to addiction and chemical imbalance. That's a compelling reason to watch myself carefully, but not a good excuse for failing to do so. I've never wanted to take medications to deal with my emotions, though I don't judge those who do. Of course I'm not a doctor, but in my view, mental problems have so many layers of complexity that drugs are more likely to mask, rather than resolve, them. I would prefer to draw on the wisdom of others, combined with my own inner strength, to work through each issue. I've also had too much experience seeing the damage that drugs and alcohol can do, both in and out of sport, to be attracted to the idea that any substance can be a solution for mental health problems. Though I enjoy the occasional social drink, I'm happy to say that I have exorcised the part of my father (and my grandfathers on both sides) that drove him to seek escape through liquor.

I like to share the things I'm learning with Peter, because I find them fascinating, and because I like receiving his input. He has a really good bullshit detector, and he understands more clearly than I do when someone is helping me or taking from me. Our relationship also helps me keep my actions in line with my mental progress. It's easy to say, "Oh, I learned this," and then to be a complete asshole by not applying that knowledge.

Since I quit sports, Peter and I have grown closer, partly because we spend more time together. Before, we shared some amazing moments and experiences, but we were so often separated that we really didn't know each other. Many of our friends joked that when we finally lived together, we might not actually like each other, but the opposite has happened. Now, every day when I look at him, I can hardly believe that this is the beautiful person with whom I'll spend the rest of my life. I keep learning new things about him and about the fantastic experiences he's had. He's always exposing me to different ways of thinking, pointing out books and articles that become important to me as well. Now when we're together, we're genuinely together, with no competing obligations hanging over me. Peter has retained the beginner's mind. He's always had a remarkable sense of wonder, which I'm learning from him. Our relationship is an eighteen-year work-in-progress. I'm so grateful that he has been patient enough to stick with me.

Peter taught me that a time would come when I would no longer have the passion to race. He was right. When it was gone, it was gone. It was good to have had someone warn me, in a positive way, that the ability to focus at a high level would abandon me, because that's what happened.

When I was a pro athlete, everything had been about me, about my training, my performance, my accidents, my recovery. Narcissism was defined as "commitment." It became an invisible cloak I was encouraged to wear. Self-absorption is hard to shake, even after there's no excuse for it. The lack of goals can lead to a different kind of narcissism: *No one suffers as much as me, no one has ever known such despair, no one had so little reason to get up in the morning.*

A few months ago, I saw some skiers performing roller skiing intervals on the steep hill near the condo Peter and I rent in Canmore, Alberta, training when they couldn't get on snow. As I watched their coaches videotaping them, I was so glad it wasn't me on that hill. What those skiers didn't realize was that all that monotonous, gruelling training is the fun part. The pain of racing is another step up. After that comes the Olympics, another very steep step, where you try to make magic happen. It's so hard.

I'm grateful that I finally found a way to pursue sport that made it about more than just winning: spending time with Joé Juneau as he taught hockey to the Inuit, travelling the world for Right to Play, joining the Bell Let's Talk program. What I want most now is to serve. To improve myself so I can share those improvements with others. That's what I want each and every day that is left to me.

That's life for me in the off-season.

23

FULL STOP

In the summer of 2013, when Peter and I were bike touring along the extensive trails that radiate around the mountain town of Rossland, B.C., I received a phone call from my mom: "It's about your dad."

He was now in special care.

"He's coughing badly," Mom told me. "He's stopped eating, and he's lost a lot of weight. I have no idea what will happen in the coming hours, or days, or weeks, for that matter."

I knew that my dad was suffering from geriatric dementia, and I panicked at the thought of my being so far away when he might be dying.

After I informed Peter, he suggested renting a car to drive to Calgary, then flying to Winnipeg.

When I phoned my mom for advice, she replied, "Your dad is in such a bad state, maybe you should just keep alive the vision of him when you saw him last."

My mom also informed me that Dad had an order to resuscitate on his file. We both knew he would not want to live without a functioning body or mind. I agreed to change that to DNR—do not resuscitate—if his heart or breathing should stop. Though it wounded me to know this decision would end his life, I was grateful to help him escape his living hell.

After I ended our phone call, I wondered what my mom had meant about my father's "bad state." Even when I'd visited him three weeks before, Mom had warned me that Kenneth Hughes, once a strapping man of six feet four, was already a shadow of his former self.

As soon as I saw him sitting on the edge of his hospital bed, I'd started crying. He smiled at me as I hugged his frail body, struggling to hold back more tears.

When I stepped out of his hug, my dad grabbed my arm. "Strong," he said, still smiling. I cried some more, glad he seemed to know who I was.

The silence in my father's room was broken by swearing and yelling and moaning throughout the ward. *How had my dad ended up here?* Of course, I knew that answer. He'd been aggressive to the home-care workers who regularly visited him. Tragically, he was now with his own kind—others who felt angry and frustrated and trapped inside failing minds and bodies.

As I walked with my father around the ward's small loop, he pointed to a locked door, then to a poster that told patients to "Know Your Rights." Even with dementia, my dad remained a rebel. He knew that locked door led to freedom, and he believed that poster gave him the right to escape. On another occasion, he pointed out a window to a bus stop. I could tell from his mischievous smile that this was phase two of his escape plan.

My dad had never been easy. When I was older, I used to say to him, "I love you, Dad," but he just said, "Yeah, yeah, yeah." He was never able to manage "I love you, too, Clara."

At one point during this visit, he did say to me, "I thought I'd lost you."

He then asked Mom, "Where's the other one?" He was referring to my sister, whom he refused to call by name because of her troubles.

We told him that Dodie, who was on a day pass from her long-term-care facility, was coming later, to which he replied, "Well, maybe we can all live here, you know, like a proper family."

This was sweet to hear, bringing me to both tears and laughter. I refrained from saying, *Yeah, well, it's a little late for that, Dad.*

The next day, he'd forgotten our previous visit. A week later, he was strapped to his bed, having forgotten who he was, and having grown violent.

After talking with my mom, Peter and I continued our B.C. bike tour, as she had suggested. A few days later, I received another call, causing me to stop on the roadside in the heat of a summer's evening.

My dad had just died. It was July 23, 2013.

He'd stopped eating as a final gesture, making his own choice about when to leave us. Even in dementia, my dad performed the last independent act he could: He engaged in a hunger strike.

I dropped my bike, then sat beside it on the grass. When Peter saw my tears, he knew what I had to tell him: "Dad has gone."

I felt gutted and confused, unable to sort out my emotions.

We climbed back onto our bikes, then pedalled the final 20 or so kilometres into Nelson, B.C. That forward motion freed me. I felt a welcome sense of relief that my father had escaped from his hospital bed, through that locked door, and onto that bus, to whatever awaited him. I also felt a grateful sense of peace, when I thought about how much my father had supported everything I had done in sport, and how he'd encouraged my relationship with Peter. While others had judged us for our unconventional, spontaneous lifestyle, my dad had fully appreciated us, especially Peter the Prince. For that, I could never thank him enough.

I still have moments of sadness, knowing he's not here anymore. In his eighty years, he affected so many people. Former students told me that my dad had changed their lives. They would say things like "Your dad was the only teacher who ever actually taught me something worthwhile." Some went on to be politicians, teachers, other professionals. The impecunious artists my dad supported by buying their work were especially grateful. They'd tell me, "I was really struggling when your dad commissioned one of my pieces. He just did it to help me."

Instead of giving handouts, my dad had encouraged creativity. He understood the intensity of the artistic process, and since he didn't have talent, he wanted to support those who did.

I believe my dad had moments in his life that he loved, and I'm happy for that. I must also admit that I'm relieved he's no longer here. I really loved him—love him still—but some of his behaviours pissed me off because of how he abused my mom and damaged my sister and me. If only he could have been the wonderful person he was capable of being to those who loved him.

I know that I can best honour Kenneth Hughes's memory by encouraging kids in the Arctic, or in other disadvantaged places, to find their dreams and to pursue their goals the way my father encouraged me. Despite my father's flaws, he instilled in me the belief that we are all equal, and that anything is possible. If I had said, "Dad, I am going to the moon," he would have replied, "Of course you are." He stirred in me the desire to be everything I could be, so that now I have something to share with others. That is my father's legacy, which I will hold dear for the remainder of my life.

CAREER HIGHLIGHTS

Olympics

6-time Olympian (1996, 2000, 2002, 2006, 2010, 2012)
2010 bronze medal, 5000 metres (speed skating)
2006 gold medal, 5000 metres (speed skating)
2006 silver medal, team pursuit (speed skating)
2002 bronze medal, 5000 metres (speed skating)
1996 bronze medal, individual road race (cycling)
1996 bronze medal, individual time trial (cycling)

World Championships

2009 silver medal, 5000 metres (speed skating)
2008 silver medal, 5000 metres (speed skating)
2005 bronze medal, 5000 metres (speed skating)
2005 silver medal, team pursuit (speed skating)
2004 gold medal, 5000 metres (speed skating)
2003 silver medal, 5000 metres (speed skating)
1995 silver medal, time trial (cycling)

Commonwealth Games (Cycling)

2002 gold medal, individual time trial
2002 bronze medal, points race
1994 silver medal, team time trial

Pan American Games (Cycling)

2003 gold medal, points race
2003 bronze medal, individual pursuit
2003 silver medal, individual time trial
1995 silver medal, individual road race
1995 bronze medal, individual time trial
1991 bronze medal, team time trial
1991 silver medal, individual pursuit

Pan American Championships (Cycling)

2011 Pan American champion, road race
2011 Pan American champion, individual time trial

World Cups (Speed Skating 2003–2010)

13 World Cup medals (3000 metres, 5000 metres, and team pursuit)

Other Notable Results

35-time Canadian National Champion, road and track cycling, and
    speed skating
2011 Tour of the Gila, overall victory (2 stage wins)
2011 Grand Prix Cycliste Gatineau time trial, 1st
2011 Mt. Hood Cycling Classic, 2nd overall (1 stage win)
2011 Cascade Cycling Classic, 3rd overall (1 stage win)
1998 Sea Otter Classic, overall victory
1997 Tour of Texas, overall victory
1996 Hewlett-Packard International Women's Challenge, 2nd overall
    (2 stage wins)

1995 Liberty Classic, Philadelphia, 1st place
1994 Tour de l'Aude Cycliste Féminin, 2nd, prologue
1994 PowerBar Women's Challenge, overall victory (1 stage win)

Awards and Honours

Honorary Witness, Truth and Reconciliation Commission, 2015
Panthéon des Sports du Québec (Quebec Sports Hall of Fame), 2014
Manitoba Sports Hall of Fame, 2012
List of Most Influential Women (Canadian Association for the Advancement of Women and Sport and Physical Activity), 2011
Canada's Sports Hall of Fame, 2010
Canada's Walk of Fame, October 2010
Flag-Bearer, Canadian Olympic Team, 2010 Vancouver
Officer of the Order of Canada, 2010
Member of the Order of Canada, 2007
International Olympic Committee Sport and the Community Award, 2006
Member of the Order of Manitoba, 2006
Sports Personality of the Year 2006 (*La Presse*)
Honorary Doctorate of Law (Universities of Manitoba, British Columbia, and Alberta; York and Thompson Rivers Universities)
Honorary Doctorate of Letters (University of New Brunswick)
#1 Sports Hero by Jack Todd (*Montreal Gazette*)

Outreach

Bell Let's Talk
Right to Play International
Clara's Big Ride
Take a Hike program
Going Off, Growing Strong

Nunavik Youth Hockey Development Program
Kangidluasuk Student Program
Rideau Hall Foundation
Randy Starkman Charitable Foundation
Thaidene Nene proposed national park

ACKNOWLEDGEMENTS

There are, quite frankly, too many individuals to thank here. If I were to go through by name the list of folks who made all that is detailed in these pages known, we'd need another book. It's safe to say I've thanked each person profusely over the years. Some are introduced to the reader; some remain in the periphery of my lived experience. To everyone who has made these moments possible: You know who you are. Once again, thank you.

To point out the support of the provincial speed-skating and cycling associations in Manitoba, Quebec, and Ontario is a must. Add to this the Canadian Olympic Committee, Sport Canada, Own the Podium, B2ten, Fondation de l'athlète d'excellence du Québec, Canadian Sport Centres in Calgary, Winnipeg, and Montreal, and Commonwealth Games Canada. These organizations allow athletes to pursue their goals of performing on the world sporting stage. They certainly made mine possible.

To the reporters who give Olympic sport attention every few years, weaving the stories of the lesser known sportsmen and sportswomen into tales that inspire Canadians from coast to coast to coast, thank you. I'd be remiss not to single out a force in this group: Randy Starkman. Without Randy, this book odyssey never would have begun. My friend, you will never be forgotten. The CBC, CBC/Radio-Canada (radio and television), CTV, and the outcast networks of Olympic coverage, thank you for your passion for storytelling, which has inspired our nation time and again.

I'd like to thank Simon & Schuster Canada for believing in this book and keeping it alive. Without Sylvia Fraser's touch, it never would have been finished.

Nothing is done alone. I am who I've grown to be because of love, encouragement, and unconditional support from my family, however disjointed we were and are. Mom, Dad, and Dodie, I love you so much. To my husband and best friend, Peter, *te amo mucho*. To my extended family, the Guzmáns: *muchas, muchas gracias*.

And last, to the people, the multitude of men and women, young and old, from all walks of life and all dispositions, who struggle with the effects of mental illness: Please know that I thank you for your bravery, your courage to share, your compassion, and your support. You are the most amazing group of people and in my mind the strongest of them all. I want to say thank you for inspiring me to never give up this fight to educate and illuminate those who don't understand the reality of this struggle.

INDEX

Open Heart, Open Mind

CLARA HUGHES

1. Throughout Clara's sporting career, she endures not only intense physical pain, but also incredible emotional instability. In your opinion, does Clara's emotionally traumatic childhood contribute to her capacity for physical endurance? How did her chaotic inner thoughts influence her focus on cycling and skating?

2. Discuss your perception of mental health before and after reading Clara's story. What have you learned through reading her memoir?

3. The ability to transition between speed skating, cycling, skating, and then back to cycling is an incredible feat of strength, dedication, and adaptability. What can we learn from Clara's willingness to start from scratch by participating in these two sports?

4. Clara realizes that much of her pain is connected to the guilt she feels about her family's dysfunction. Though some of this pain is mitigated by helping others, ultimately Clara must let go of her sense of responsibility for her family members. Are you or is someone you know struggling with a similar situation?

5. As the title suggests, readers are welcomed into the inner workings of Clara's heart and mind. What is your opinion about being so publicly honest? How will learning about Clara's inner and outer struggles benefit her readership?

6. In the "permanent off-season" after her retirement, Clara had to overcome restlessness, anxiety, and severe self-doubt while learning how to be happy without the distraction of competitive sport. She has found relative peace by finding ways to give back and connect with others, but most importantly, she has come to terms with the fact that her medals and accomplishments, while a huge part of her life, do not define her. What does Clara represent to you, aside from her successful sporting career?

7. Though Clara loved professional cycling and skating and has won medals in both sports, she finds many of her happiest moments exploring trails and wilderness parks by herself or with her husband, Peter. Where is the place you are the happiest? Why are you happiest there?

8. Clara has had significant struggles with substance abuse and body image issues in her life, in large part because of her turbulent upbringing and demanding career. Her psychological breakthrough in 2007 with Owen Schwartz helped her realize how she could heal, but she still deals with the difficulties of her mental state every day. What do you think the bird that appeared in Clara's regression therapy meant to her?

9. Clara has stressed that her proudest moments occurred when she was helping others, whether through Right to Play, Bell Canada's Let's Talk, or her contribution to various other outreach programs. When have you been most proud of yourself? How important to you is sharing your accomplishments with others?